MW01166508

101 WAYS TO TURN YOUR BUSINESS GREEN

658.4083 Min
Mintzer, Richard.
101 ways to turn your
 business green #225873684

MAR 2 4 2009

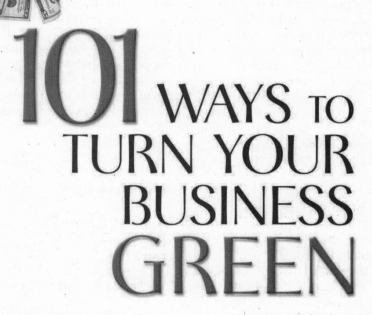

101 WAYS TO TURN YOUR BUSINESS GREEN

The Business Guide to Eco-Friendly Profits

RICH MINTZER

E P
Entrepreneur Press

Publisher: Jere L. Calmes
Editorial Development and Production: CWL Publishing Enterprises, Inc.,
Madison, WI, www.cwlpub.com
Cover Design by David Shaw

Copyright © 2008 by Entrepreneur Media Inc. All rights reserved.

Reproduction or translation of any part of this work beyond that permitted
by Section 107 or 108 of the 1976 United States Copyright Act without
permission of the copyright owner is unlawful. Requests for permission or
further information should be addressed to the Business Products Division, Entrepreneur Media Inc.

This publication is designed to provide accurate and authoritative information in regard to the subject matter covered. It is sold with the understanding that the publisher is not engaged in rendering legal, accounting,
or other professional services. If legal advice or other expert assistance is
required, the services of a competent professional person should be
sought.

> —From a Declaration of Principles jointly adopted by
> a Committee of the American Bar Association and
> a Committee of Publishers and Associations

ISBN 13: 978-1-59918-263-6
      10: 1-59918-263-7

Library of Congress Cataloging-in-Publication Data

Mintzer, Richard.
  101 ways to turn your business green / by Rich Mintzer.
    p. cm.
  Includes index.
  ISBN 1-59918-263-7 (alk. paper)
  1. Management—Environmental aspects. 2. Business enterprises—
Environmental aspects. I. Title.
  HD30.255.M56 2008
  658.4'083—dc22

                                                2008030977

Printed in Canada.

12 11 10 09 08   10 9 8 7 6 5 4 3 2 1

Entrepreneur Press is proud to announce that this book was produced with
the use of 100 percent post-consumer FSC-certified recycled paper made
from 100 percent old growth forest-free and acid-free components,
processed chlorine-free and printed with vegetable-based inks.

Contents

Preface	*ix*
Section 1. Embrace the Basics	**1**
1. Embrace Green	3
2. Make a Time Commitment for Greening Your Business	5
3. Start With an Energy Audit	7
4. Decrease Your Carbon Footprint	10
5. Design Your Office in an Eco-Friendly Manner	11
6. Become an Eco-Friendly Shopper	14
7. Start an Office Recycling Program	16
8. Know Your Plastics (and Sort by Number)	17
Section 2. Tangibles	**21**
9. Institute a Green Purchasing Policy	23
10. Use Green Office Supplies	24
11. Use Energy-Efficient Appliances	26
12. Switch to Energy-Efficient Lighting	28
13. Upgrade and Maintain Your HVAC System	30
14. Insulate Your Facility Properly	32
15. Insulate or Replace Windows and Doors	34
16. Quick Tip: Buy Air Conditioner and Vent Covers	36
17. Quick Tip: Pool Your Office Resources	37
18. Pool Your Resources With Other Homebased Business Owners	38
19. Create a Green Home Office	40
20. Quick Tip: Green Up Your Bathroom	42
Section 3. Natural and Renewable Energy	**43**
21. Explore Passive Solar Heating and Cooling	45
22. Consider a "Cool" Green Roof	47
23. Quick Tip: Try Chilled Beams	49
24. Go Solar	50

Contents

25. Use Wind Turbine Power   52
26. Install Eco-Friendly Flooring   54

Section 4. Water Conservation   57
27. Start a "Save Water" Program   59
28. Install a Water Filtration System   61
29. Utilize Rainwater   63
30. Use Indoor Plants as Natural Air Filters   65

Section 5. Paper and Printing (and Signage)   67
31. Start a Paper Waste Prevention Program   69
32. Switch to Green Printing   71
33. Use Greener Signage   73

Section 6. Greener Packaging, Design, and Packing   75
34. Implement Sustainable Packaging Policies   77
35. Minimize and Redesign Your Packaging   79
36. Use Eco-Friendly Packaging Labels   81
37. Use Eco-Friendly Packing Materials   83
38. Consider Reusable Bags Over Plastic or Paper   85

Section 7. Technology   89
39. Switch to Energy-Efficient Computer Use   91
40. When Buying New Computers, Buy Greener Models   92
41. Start a Company-Wide Computer/Cartridge E-Cycling Program   96
42. Quick Tip: Switch to E-Signatures   98
43. Recycle Cell Phones for the Planet and for Charity   99
44. Quick Tip: Use Rechargeable Batteries   101
45. Quick Tip: Go With Voice Mail   102

Section 8. Less Waste and a Cleaner Work Environment   105
46. Have a Waste Audit Done   107
47. Quick Tip: Reduce Holiday Party Waste   108
48. Consider Composting   109
49. Share Your Waste   111
50. Start an Anti-Litter Campaign   113
51. Clean Green   114
52. Maintain a High Level of Indoor Air Quality   116
53. Stop Junk Mail From Coming to Your Office   118

Section 9. Shipping and Products   121
54. Work With Green Vendors and Suppliers   123
55. Quick Tip: Avoid Shipping Air   125
56. Work With Local Suppliers   127
57. Make Your Internal Shipping Needs Greener   128
58. Minimize Excess Inventory   129
59. Revamp Your Products—Get Greener   131
60. Think Bio-Plastics   134

Section 10. Transportation, Travel and Telecommuting   137
61. Make the Switch to Flex Fuel or Hybrid Cars,
    Vans, and Trucks   139
62. Think Green Tires   142
63. Get Environmental Roadside Assistance and
    Use Green Travel Services   143
64. Encourage Alternative Forms of Commuting   145
65. Create More Telecommuting Opportunities   147
66. Think Greener Business Travel   150
67. Offset Business Travel with Green Tags   152

Section 11. Intangibles   155
68. Change the Coffee Culture in Your Office   157
69. Quick Tip: Hold Greener Meetings   58
70. Create a Green Team   159
71. Produce a Sustainability Report   161
72. Hire a Director of Sustainability   163
73. Establish a Consumer Recycling Program   165
74. Dress Greener   167

Section 12. Putting Your Best Foot Forward   169
75. Use Green Marketing and Promotion   171
76. Embrace Word-of-Mouth Marketing   174
77. Conduct Surveys to Gauge Your Customers'
    Interest in the Environment   176
78. Quick Tip: Minimize the Media Blitz   178

Section 13. Locations, Locations, and Greener Locations   181
79. Consider Moving Into a Green Office Building   183
80. Expanding Your Facility? Build Green   186
81. Moving Part II: Consider a Brownfield   188

Contents

82. Maintain Some Green Acreage   191
83. Consider Downsizing   192

**Section 14. Social Responsibility and Doing Better
         for Your People   195**
84. Start a Program of Company-Wide Volunteer Hours   197
85. Support and Sponsor Environmental
     Groups and Causes   198
86. Become a Role Model: Educate Others
     on Sustainability   201
87. Become the Green Center for Your Community   203
88. Produce a Green Newsletter   204
89. Lobby for Green   205
90. Attract Green Employees   207
91. Treat Your Employees to Wellness   209
92. Quick Tip: Gift Green   210
93. Go Organic   211
94. Quick Tip: Create a Company Library   213
95. Provide Green Incentives   214
96. Look for Transparency in Certifications
     and Ecolabels   215
97. Consider Socially Responsible Investing   217
98. Buy Carbon Offsets   220

Section 15. Some Final Suggestions   223
99. Rate Your Own Corporate Citizenship   225
100. Teach Future Generations   227
101. Don't Stop   228

Section 16. Putting It All Together   231

Appendix A. Glossary   235

Appendix B. Resources   241

Index   247

Preface

So, you want to join the legions of greener companies and become part of the future of business practices and protocol. Sustainable practices are not at all difficult, and if numerous business owners all take the same environmentally conscious steps that you plan to take, then together, you can make a huge difference. The problem facing so many entrepreneurs is where to begin.

In this book, we provide 101 recommendations to make your business greener. Some of the suggestions are simple, such as buying rechargeable batteries, post-consumer recycled paper products, or nontoxic, organic cleaning products. Other recommendations require making a larger commitment to change, such as opting for passive solar heating, or having more staffers telecommute when possible. And, there are larger-scale changes possible, too, which might include utilizing renewable energy by installing solar panels or using wind turbines for power, or moving to a greener office building. Obviously, these are not commitments every business can make, but they can certainly remain future possibilities when you and your business are in a position to make such major changes.

Touching All the Bases

The key to going greener is thinking greener, and today many people are already in the environmentally responsible mindset. It may be easier than you think to get everyone in your company onboard. As you start reading the 101 ways, you'll find some of the basics up-front to get you off and running. Just as every diet needs to begin with a healthy meal plan, your plan to go green should also start off with a few of these basics, such as an energy audit, a recycling plan, and the commitment to become an eco-friendly shopper, which means taking a few extra moments to look at labels and packaging.

As you read through the wide range of suggestions, you will

Preface

note that we start off with some clear-cut, tangible energy-saving tips that can easily be implemented in your business office, store, factory, or home office. For example, you can switch to energy-efficient lighting and buy Energy Star appliances. You can also learn to pool resources, so you can limit some of the tangible items you need to purchase.

You will see options for renewable energy such as passive solar cooling, wind turbines, and solar panels, all of which can lower those high heating bills while benefiting Mother Earth. We also touch on saving water, not wasting paper, and using soy-based ink when printing.

Sustainable packaging is a very important topic today, and we offer suggestions that include package redesign and shipping. Then it's on to technology and waste. Learn what you can do to green your computer use and what to do with your computers after they have served their purpose.

Greener travel, hybrid cars, and alternative means of commuting are also gaining favor, and we have included them in a section on transportation, travel, and telecommuting.

Along with environmental concerns, going greener today also means taking responsibility for social change and doing more for the health and well-being of your employees and the community at large. From working with charities to treating your staff to wellness days to providing green incentives, the section on greater good looks at the human aspect of going green, social responsibility, and even socially responsible investing.

We hope that as you read through *101 Ways to Turn Your Business Green*, you'll highlight certain suggestions, fold down the corners of the pages, or create markers to indicate recommendations that are environment-friendly possibilities for your business now or in the future. The size of your business, finances, people power, location, type of business, and the industry that you are in will all factor into your decisions regarding which of the 101 suggestions to implement. It's safe to say, that if you start with 5 to 10 changes, you will be making significant strides forward in going greener. You will

see how your efforts can save you money—which means an opportunity for a greater profit margin—and help build your customer base
since consumers today are very green-minded.

Acknowledgments

I'd like to thank a number of people who provided marvelous information for this book, including Steven D. Strauss from MrAllbiz.com,
Karel Samsom Ph.D., Byron Kennard at the Center for Small Business
and the Environment, Ron King from the National Insulation Association, Joshua Onysko from Pangea Organics, and also Sara Good for
her assistance; Bruce Nordham at CuttingPaper.com, Meghan O'Neill
from Treehugger.com, and Bryan Hughes for his help; Greg Owsley
at New Belgium Brewery and Brian Simpson for his help; Mark
Parnes from the law firm of Wilson, Sonsini, Goodrich & Rosati, Kelly
LaPlante from Kelly LaPlante Organic Designs, Anne Bedarf at
GreenBlue.org and Erin Malec for her help; Paul McGrath of
Ridespring.com, Darrin C. Duber-Smith of Green Marketing, Kevin
Tuerff from Enviromedia, Eric Newman from Newman Building
Designs, Kate Torgerson and Elysa Hammond from ClifBar; Roger
Strong at Solar Wind Works, Alex Szabo from thegreenoffice.com,
insulation consultant Ron King, John Jordan at Principor Communi-
cations; environmental journalist and author Trish Riley, Robert
Colangelo of the National Brownfield Association and publisher of
Brownfield News, Lewis Buchner at Eco Timber, Annette Racond
from Wellness Track, Avery Marder from Trademark Graphics, Dave
Lipschitz for his usual computer help, and of course my editor Court-
ney Thurman and the one and only Jere Calmes who believed in this
project from the start.

Embrace the Basics

1 *Embrace Green*

There are numerous suggestions throughout this book (100 more to be precise) that will help you turn your business green, make it sustainable, or environmentally friendly. Whatever you call it, you can follow the examples, use the referenced websites and make the changes to become a greener business. There are volumes of material online, in libraries, and in bookstores that explain the greenhouse effect, pollution, and global warming and include all of the other need-to-know data that presents one overwhelming argument in favor of helping the planet now and for future generations. In fact, simply renting and watching Al Gore's movie, *An Inconvenient Truth*, can provide eye-opening support for going green.

None of this great volume of gathered data, however, can hit home unless you embrace the concept (and the fact) that this is no longer the whim of a few scientists or ecology fanatics, but a very real, truly global crisis that needs the attention of all business owners, including you.

Sure, your small or midsize business has been running well, and you do not want to tamper with success. And yes, it's true that you will not make the same carbon impact upon the earth as a multibillion-dollar corporation. BUT, since more than 80 percent of businesses in the United States are of the small to midsize-business variety, together, these business owners can make a significant difference. The key is getting onboard, if for no one else, for your customers or clients, many of whom are becoming environmentally savvy and want to deal with businesses that believe as they do. Surveys routinely show that more and more people are doing business with companies that have similar beliefs to their own, and that environmental and socially responsible companies are reaping greater rewards.

Section 1. Embrace the Basics

Your first step in embracing a greener business is to understand that the overall goal isn't just to plant trees, save water, or eat organic foods, but to recognize that earth's bounties are being used up, worn out, and polluted at a rate that is dangerous for the next generation. While science has found ways to extend life, we have also jeopardized the environment. The idea of becoming sustainable is simply giving back what is being taken from the earth, replenishing it, and leaving the earth in the same condition that you found it. That is what it means to be green: to ensure the lifeline of the products you use, sell, and/or manufacture from the earth, are returned to the earth in a sustainable manner.

Take Your First Steps

First, start by taking a look at your current business practices and make a mental or written list (on recyclable paper) of the areas in which you believe you are wasting energy, polluting the environment, or acting in a socially irresponsible manner. What are your current business practices and how, if you were a greener company, would you change your methods of conducting business to be more environmentally sensitive?

What changes can you make that would set the wheels in motion to become an environmentally conscious business and at what cost?

To embrace the concept of becoming a greener business, you need to dedicate your efforts across the board to making changes that are both practical for your business, cost-effective, and sustainable. Unlike the desire to leave your mark on the business world, or make a mark in your industry, you are trying to avoid leaving a mark on the planet. Can you run a business that leaves the planet the same as if your business was never there? That's the challenge you need to embrace to grow a highly successful business, that is not at the expense of the earth.

Embrace the concept and read on to see 100 practical ways to re-color your business a shade of green.

2 Make a Time Commitment for Greening Your Business

While it may not sound like much, and does not have the green technology of solar panels or the immediate results of a deskside recycling system, the commitment to make the time for sustainability is one of the earliest and most significant steps you can take toward becoming a green business.

The majority of surveys indicate that time and budget constraints are the two primary reasons why individuals and companies do not implement a more environmentally conscious lifestyle or approach to business. In some cases, it is difficult to meet the budgetary needs of certain green programs. However, there are many low-budget, cost-effective steps that can be taken, such as passive solar power, to enhance the green contribution of your company.

Time is something we all have. It is a precious commodity, that if used correctly, can allow us to make a significant difference with the goals and accomplishments we choose to strive toward. The entrepreneur who takes the time to work diligently on a business plan, is utilizing his or her time to build a forthcoming business and subsequently, can meet their goals. Likewise, the company that sets out to become a greener entity must utilize time efficiently to make environmental goals a reality.

The question is not: Do you have the time to go green? but, rather: Will you make the time commitment to go green?

Sustainable business models all point to a team effort and a group approach. This may mean sacrificing a lunch hour or two each week, or a few hours after work, to help take part in the planning and implementation of green initiatives. It may mean simply taking those extra few seconds to shut off the air conditioner, open a window, rid your computer of your energy gobbling screen saver, set your printer to print on both sides of the page, or wash your dish or

Section 1. Embrace the Basics

mug in the lunch room rather than tossing a plastic plate or Styrofoam cup into the trash. From changing the many minuscule habits that take a few extra seconds to taking part in a company-wide plan to become greener, there needs to be a conscious commitment to slow down just long enough to think sustainability.

For a business owner, the commitment to larger projects, such as switching to a solar energy source or shopping for a hybrid company car, needs to be factored into the agenda and considered a long-term means of energy and cost savings.

Time can be broken down into the next five seconds, minutes, hours, or days, or it can be looked at over a course of the next five, ten, or fifteen years. Any entrepreneur who believes in his or her business, will want to set a strategy in place for years to come. This means taking the time now, so in the year 2015, you are not an antiquated business trying to keep pace with an environmentally-advanced world. A marvelous example of planning for the future (or not) comes from a music trade magazine of the 1970s. The publishers did not embrace the new technology and preliminary electronic games and gadgets of the early 1980s. Competing publications, however, did start setting pages aside to grow with the advent of computers, video games, and such technology. The resistant magazine, very soon found that far more advertisers turned to their competition, and as a result, the magazine was left behind and ultimately had to close their doors.

While the motivation for saving the environment should not be to keep pace with your competitors, the frank truth of the matter is, that whether you wish to move forward or not, the environmental movement is not a passing fad, but the wave of the coming generation. It behooves the business owners of today to schedule a few extra meetings to address such issues.

Some businesses have regularly scheduled weekly meetings to address environmental concerns, while others have a specific committee or task force in place to study the feasibility of environmental projects and make recommendations and online reports. In some cases, if the budget allows, an energy consultant or staff ecologist may be hired who can then set up specific times for meetings at which he or she can lay out a plan. In all cases, time must be worked into the schedules of everyone involved, and it starts by a commitment from the top.

If business owners can sacrifice a round of golf or consolidate any of the host of weekly meetings to make time to address environmental issues, the ball will start rolling, and you can begin putting new systems in place for a greener business.

3 Start With an Energy Audit

One of the first steps toward becoming greener is to determine exactly how much energy you are using now and at what cost.

You can start with a simple energy audit. To begin, you will want to review your own energy expenditure and measure it on an ongoing basis by reading your energy bills and meters. Then, as your business grows and expands, you will be able to account for the additional energy consumption and measure the increase by additional units of production or by additional hours. This way you can see if you are maintaining a stable amount of energy use in conjunction with your growth. Of course, you will also want to compare your energy use with the needs of similar businesses. This will take some research, but will provide a benchmark, so you will know what a business of your size (and type) should be using in your geographic location.

For more precise results, you can have an audit conducted by an outside auditor. Audits may be done by local utilities, energy efficiency experts, or consultants, who can evaluate your energy use and punch up the numbers, so you can see where you can save money and as a result, help the environment. For a small business, such an audit is usually completed with one on-site.

Section 1. Embrace the Basics

An energy audit should review many aspects of your business, including the construction of the facility and how much energy is escaping through structural deficits or through poor insulation. In addition, heating and cooling systems are taken into account to determine how effective they are and how much energy is being spent to maintain these systems. Water heating equipment can also be a major drain on energy, along with lighting, which is typically not well-managed in most businesses, particularly in offices. All machinery is reviewed, from computers to kitchen appliances, to determine if there are energy-saving features or possible Energy Star appliances that can be purchased as replacements. Finally, windows and doors are also taken into account, again, to see if they are contributing to wasted energy. Poorly insulated doors and windows can be a source of unwanted cool or warm air.

An energy audit will result in a report that lists your energy expenses and charts those numbers over time. The consultant, or energy analyst, should be able to provide you with comparable numbers for other businesses of your size in your geographic area, since varying climates will affect the need for energy use. Such a detailed analysis will allow you to compare yourself to nearby businesses in your industry, with many of the same energy needs.

Taking Action

The next step is to reconcile your theoretical energy consumption with that shown on your actual energy bills. After analyzing your specific needs and use of lighting, heating, air conditioning, machinery, and office equipment (including computers) to determine energy efficiency, you can seek lower-cost solutions, as well as change bad habits, and adopt new company-wide business policies to decrease your energy output.

The resulting suggestions can range from structural building repairs, to using LED light bulbs, minimizing paper use, and buying insulation blankets for water pipes. The bottom line is that an energy audit is a starting point from which to build a plan that can save both energy consumption and lower business costs. It can be your guiding "proclamation" from which you become greener and save a significant amount of money in the long term.

The problem is that not all local energy companies provide audit services and consultants can be difficult to find. Since audits are not uniformly available, Energy Star offers a software program to help you do your own assessment. Energy Star is a joint program of the U.S. Environmental Protection Agency and the U.S. Department of Energy, designed to help protect the environment through energy-efficient products and practices. In 2007, Energy Star-rated products and guidelines saved American home owners and businesses $16 billion dollars on their utility bills, while making a significant impact on the global warming crisis. Top performing businesses are recognized annually and accredited by Energy Star.

The Energy Star Interactive Management Program, called Portfolio Manager, tells you where your entire business stands, energy-wise (or your entire building, if you own it) once you provide all of your utility billing data for the past 24 months on an Excel-type spreadsheet. Once you enter your gas, electricity, water usage, and other operating characteristics of your company, or building (based on your zip code), the program will tell you what your usage should amount to for a given year, calculating regional weather patterns into the equation. The program can compare your energy usage and subsequent payments from one year to the next. It you are part of a trade organization, you can also share the data with other affiliated members, if you so choose. Finally, the software program allows you to rate your energy performance on a scale of 1–100, relative to similar buildings nationwide. The password-protected file ensures privacy and is not linked to any database. For more on Portfolio Manager, you can go to **energystar.gov**. You can also call **1-888-STAR-YES** (1-888-782-7937) for more information during regular business hours.

4 Decrease Your Carbon Footprint

A carbon footprint, or imprint, is a measure of carbon dioxide or CO_2 emitted into the atmosphere by humans and/or businesses conducting routine activities. At its most comprehensive, a carbon footprint measures the impact of products from their creation to their final disposal by the consumer.

Many businesses limit this cycle to monitoring the amount of carbon dioxide emitted through the combustion of fossil fuels, in (only) the daily operation of the business itself. This is not the entire picture, but it does, at least, capture some measure of the energy waste from the production process. The goal is for a company to be carbon neutral, meaning no (zero) emissions through activities, or paying offsetting fees for whatever is emitted.

Much like energy audits, a company's carbon imprint can be determined and measured by calculating specific information about emissions from factories, machinery, and vehicles used within the course of doing business. Energy use, miles driven, consumer behavior, and other factors are brought together and calculated to result in a measure known as a carbon footprint.

You can do this with any business. If, for example, you took a lemonade stand and calculated that it takes x amount of petroleum to grow the lemons, x amount of petroleum to bring the lemons in to the stand, x amount of petroleum to make the cups, x amount of petroleum to generate the lighting to work at night, and so on, you would be calculating the entire process or lifeline. "Generally, there is a lot more to include into the equation than most companies are using to calculate their footprint. Ultimately, the corporate footprint globally is $x+y=z$ and the goal is then to offset z," explains Joshua Onysko, president and founder of Pangea Organics, a Boulder Colorado-based maker of organic skincare and body care products and a company with a zero carbon footprint.

Many companies can be used to offset a carbon footprint, such as purchasing wind credits or offset credits. "The reality is that at first a company should be looking at reducing, reusing and recycling. You always want to make the first attempt to lessen your own impact," adds Onysko.

Many of the means of making your business greener, as mentioned throughout this book, will lower the carbon footprint or imprint. As is typically the case, there are some energy needs that you cannot do without and those that you can only lower to a manageable level and still be a profitable business. The goal is to examine as many aspects of the product life cycle as possible, and see where you can make changes.

There are a few carbon calculators available online which can help you get started on this task. Take some time and punch in the numbers.

- ♻ EPA, at **epa.gov**
- ♻ The Nature conservancy at **nature.org**
- ♻ Carbonfund at **carbonfund.org/site/pages/ carbon_calculators**

5 Design Your Office in an Eco-Friendly Manner

"Green design follows the same principles as other interior design except that everything you do, every step of the way, you are considering the earth and its resources," says Kelly LaPlante of Kelly LaPlante Organic Design located in Venice Beach, California.

For many businesses, going greener begins with the setting in which people spend numerous hours each day working. It is from here that your company-wide green mindset can begin with a new greener design.

It is a matter of thinking green with each step of the design process. For example, if you are painting, you are still going to

Section 1. Embrace the Basics

choose the color that you want, but you will be looking for a low or no VOC paint (Volatile Organic Compound). Another example might be in furniture. If you are having a piece of furniture made, instead of using polyurethane foam for the core of the cushion, you can explore different options, such as organic latex. For businesses, this generally comes into play when moving to a new office or redecorating your current facilities. Of course one aspect of remodeling, moving, or redecorating, is finding other ways in which to reuse your old furnishings or recycle them. In some situations, employees get permission to take old desks or other discarded office furniture home for reuse in some practical or decorative manner.

LaPlante recommends first looking at what you can reuse. "One misconception that people have is that they have to throw away everything because it's not green and start completely from scratch. In reality, one of the greenest things you can do is reuse what you have in some manner because it takes no new resources," explains LaPlante, who is now in her tenth year of green design.

Another major factor in greening your office occurs when you upgrade your carpeting. There are a number of carpet companies that make carpets out of recycled polyester, saving a product from going to a landfill. This is not only recycled, but it is recyclable, so it can be recycled at the next remodeling. A company called InterFace (**interfaceflor.com**) has perfected carpet tiles, which are now very chic. "The beauty of carpet tiles, is that if something happens to the rug, which is not uncommon in a busy office, you can replace just that section. You can take it, recycle it, and replace it rather than having to replace a full room of carpeting," says LaPlante, who also recommends natural air from windows that actually open. Good ventilation helps ensure that the new carpet or new paint smell will not linger, giving employees headaches over the next several months or even years. Fresh air and airflow can do wonders for office employees from a health perspective. More people maintain good health and take fewer sick days, when the air quality is good. Indoor air quality is also of concern from a green and health standpoint, as is natural lighting.

An increasing number of furnishings are made from wood certified by the FSC, the Forest Stewardship Counsel. The FSC is a third party company that makes sure no habitats are destroyed when logging wood for certified furniture, and that the employees responsible for its manufacture are receiving appropriate pay for their work. They certify wood products that are eco-friendly and from socially responsible sources. You can find FSC certified oak, mahogany, or other woods that have been sustainably managed in their production. Bamboo is also a very renewable resource, provided it has not been coated with a dye or that formaldehyde has not been used on it. If you are using bamboo, or any FSC wood, make sure it was not treated with chemicals after it was FSC-certified.

The best thing about recycled fabrics is that they were put back through the system and recycled, accordingly. "Many recycled fabrics are also very durable which is important for offices," adds LaPlante, who provides more information at **kellylaplante.com**.

Check to see that all materials meet fire codes.

Finally, if you are looking for the latest in eco-friendly chairs, Herman Miller offers a new chair made of primarily recycled materials that is also ergonomic. Knoll also offers Greenguard-certified office furnishings. If you can't reuse what you already have, then these are some environmentally friendly products.

While looking for new eco-friendly office furnishings, you should also consider helping limit gas use and emissions by looking at local manufacturers and distributors. Less shipping is a plus, especially if your new furniture comes directly from the manufacturer and does not need to be routed through a warehouse.

There are many factors that go into greener furnishings. These are just a sample of the many items to consider when designing, or re-designing, a greener office.

6 Become an Eco-Friendly Shopper

Business owners, including those selling retail or wholesale products and/or services, can become greener shoppers, themselves. Environmentally Preferable Purchasing (EPP) as it's called, means buying products with a reduced negative effect on the environment rather than competing products serving the same purpose. This doesn't mean you should go out of your way to find what you need, but that you can simply order products more selectively. For example, most of the paper needs for your business can be recycled. This holds true with most office products, so you'll need to make identifying recycled products part of your shopping routine, much the way that dieters look at calories and anyone with high cholesterol should be looking at the trans fat content.

There are two types of recycled products you will find. Post-consumer recycled products, which are those that have been used by consumers and then recycled, and post-manufacturer recycled, which is waste created by a manufacturing process that is subsequently used as a constituent in another manufacturing process. While post-consumer waste is preferable, both are means of recycling.

Look closely at office supplies, cleaning products, equipment, and everything else you typically need to buy for your business and see if there is a greener version. To make your search easier, you can look for products that meet Green Seal standards and have their certificates. Visit **greenseal.org** for more information.

Other shopping considerations may include:

- Patronize companies that feature green business practices.
- Shop locally to minimize long distance shipping.
- Look for products that are more durable and will last longer.
- Select products that do not drain energy or waste water, such as Energy Star appliances (as discussed throughout this book).

⟳ Attempt to reuse what you have before buying something new.

⟳ Buy products from suppliers who do not use excessive or non-biodegradable packaging. If you don't know what type of materials a company uses for shipping, ask. Say no to Styrofoam peanuts and bubble wrap. You can also stop ordering from suppliers that send products with excess paper, such as shipments with cardboard dividers between the bottles, or excessive plastic or shrink-wrap.

⟳ Reuse shipping materials. Just as kids love to turn the boxes their toys come in into new houses and places to hide, you can also reuse boxes.

When you are shopping in a brick and mortar store, take along your own cloth bags rather than use the paper or plastic bags provided by the store.

In a land of excess, we also need to refocus our shopping mentality to eliminate overbuying. It will save you money and allow you to more easily make a profit rather than load up your stockroom or storeroom. Businesses routinely buy at least 30 percent more supplies and equipment than they actually need, and this does not include excess inventory. Determine where you can cut corners and, if you do overbuy, let someone else use or buy your excess rather than waste it.

Becoming a green shopper for your business, or training your office manager, plant manager, or chief purchasing agent to think sustainable and eco-friendly, just takes time and practice. As you'll see in many of the suggestions throughout the book, it all starts with the right mindset.

7 Start an Office Recycling Program

Whether your business employs three people or three hundred, an office committed to recycling is a very basic green step you can take to enhance your commitment to the environment.

Of course, if you develop waste reduction policies first, you can limit your recyclables from the start. For example, if reusable mugs are used for coffee, you'll have fewer disposable coffee cups to recycle. Nonetheless, recycling is part and parcel to green office etiquette today, or at least it should be. To begin with, you'll want to have one or more people oversee such a program, depending on how large your staff is. The first step is identifying what is recyclable, such as newspapers, office paper, glass and plastic bottles, aluminum cans, and cardboard boxes. Make a list. If you run an auto repair business, or have a fleet of vehicles (or even a few), old tires can be recycled and ultimately reused as doormats and playground safety covering.

The next step is to find a local recycling pickup service. Via the internet or phonebook you will find companies listed under waste disposal and/or recycling.

For computer cartridges and technical equipment, you will usually find separate recycling services. Recycling vendors have different rates and specific rules and regulations they follow, some in conjunction with local ordinances. There may be certain days on which they make pickups in your area and specific places from which they can pick up. You can ask them how they expect recyclable material to be collected. For example, old newspaper usually needs to be bundled and cardboard boxes should be broken down.

You can also contact local recycling centers, many of which can be found at **recyclingcenters.org**. Centers in every state are listed on the site.

Next, you'll need to find a place within your office in which to collect these items. This can range from one central location in a smaller office to desk-side recycling in large companies. Depending on the size of your facility, you can determine how many bins you may need and situate them accordingly. Typically, most offices have bins for paper, plastic, bottles, and cans.

You will need someone to collect and put the recyclables out for pickup, or take them to a recycling center, typically once per week. Such collection can be on a rotating schedule in an office with 20 or more people, so that different volunteers are responsible and no one person has the same task each week.

Finally, spreading the word among employees is important to make sure everyone gets with the program. As a business owner or manager, you can set the tone (by example). If your staff sees you are determined to go green, they will follow, if for no other reason than because they want to stay on your good side. You can also provide incentives for your employees, collectively, for recycling and meeting specific goals and/or individually, for those who have volunteered to spearhead the effort. For more recycling information, you might check out Earth 911 at **earth911.org/recycling.**

> **FAST FACT**
> Making a can out of recycled aluminum takes only 5 percent of the energy needed to make an aluminum can from raw materials.

8 Know Your Plastics (and Sort by Number)

At present, not all plastics are easily recyclable, no matter what the label says. There isn't much of a market for the lower grades of plastic, making them more difficult to recycle. To make life simpler for those of us concerned about recycling, you can check the grade number of the plastic, usually found within the three arrow label indicating that the product is recyclable. The higher grades, which are the lower numbers, such as 1 and 2, are the more commonly recyclable plastics. This isn't to say that other grades of plastic will not be recycled. However, there are more recycling centers available for Grade 1, Polyethylene Terephthalate (PET) and Grade 2, High-Density Polyethylene (HDP) plastics. Soda bottles are typically made from Grade 1 and bottles for milk and water from Grade 2. Grade 3 is Polyvinyl chloride (which can be toxic in production and disposal); Grade 4, Low Density Polyethylene; Grade 5, Polypropylene; Grade 6, Polystrene; and Grade 7, a composite of any plastics that do not fall into the above categories.

Sorting plastics can be beneficial and also separating lids to be collected separately is recommended, since often the lids are not made from the same grade of plastic as the container. Many recycling companies do not want the lids because they cannot be recycled with the other plastic. It is also advantageous to separate Grades 1 and 2 bottles from other containers, since it is easier for most recycling companies to handle bottles, but not all can handle containers. In fact, some containers, even of high-grade plastic, may not be accepted and may be best used to store goods at home or carry lunches to and from work.

Right now, many recycling centers do not accept grades above 2, largely because there is not enough demand for such plastics, since they may have had additives contaminating them, or they may simply not be durable enough for adequate reuse.

FAST FACT

Apparently, we are a culture hooked on plastic bottles. Did you know that in any one given hour, Americans go through 2.5 million plastic bottles?

FYI: Grade 4 plastics can be made into shampoo bottles and/or shopping bags. Grade 5 plastics are often made into fibers that can be recycled into garments, although there is limited equipment available to do this. Grade 6 plastics include Styrofoam, which, thus far has been difficult to recycle.

Since there are potential uses for these grades of plastic, as technology advances, we will hopefully see more recycling centers accepting them. For now, look for Grades 1 and 2 plastics, then sort and recycle. To read more on plastics, and find a nationwide list of recycling centers, go to **plasticresources.com**.

Tangibles

9 Institute a Green Purchasing Policy

I f a policy comes from the top, it's likely to stick. With that in mind, why not institute a green purchasing policy? This is where you list some of the criteria for purchasing supplies and equipment that will be used throughout your business. Of course, not everything you purchase can be green, so you will have to balance some conventional purchasing with the green criteria. "You want to provide a clear set of policy directions to people who will be implementing the program," says Alex Szabo, founder and CEO of **Thegreenoffice.com**, where thousands of office products are carefully evaluated using 50 criteria and then categorized from green to light green to conventional, providing a one-stop shop for office supplies.

The key is to know what you are looking for when purchasing equipment and supplies, and with that in mind, Szabo notes some categories on which to focus. "Compostable and biodegradable products, those that have reduced chemical content with respect to competitive products, and those that have earned legitimate third-party certification," are four categories to include in such criteria, explains Szabo.

Of course, within any category there is green and greener. For example, 100 percent recycled paper typically means post-industrial, which is a positive because it means that materials otherwise wasted are being utilized for new products. However, 100 percent post-consumer recycled paper is even better, because it means that the lifeline of the product is being extended, which is the mark of sustainability.

Along with determining how to evaluate and buy greener products, you'll need to determine where you are going to shop. By using online office supply businesses such as **Thegreenoffice.com**, you can immediately eliminate the fuel used to go to and from a store or several stores.

Section 2. Tangibles

However, when buying online, you'll want to determine how far the shipping will be and the "greenness" of the website. Some of the big box stores are carrying more green products, but many are still relying predominantly on the non-green or light green offerings. Buying as much as possible at one location saves on shipping, traveling and, typically, time. Therefore, it is worthwhile to research the greenest alternatives that can cover most of your supply and equipment needs.

Of course, price points and practicality need to be considerations of your purchasing policy. Not everything will have an environmental alternative and for those items, you can consider buying carbon offsets from a reputable seller. (Find information on carbon offsets in Subsection 98.) Think green first and carbon offsets second, in an effort to counterbalance those important non-green items.

And finally, another important part of a green purchasing policy is when to buy. Can a current product serve another purpose? Can you last a little longer with last year's model? Can you reuse your paper supply before ordering more? Within your purchasing policy, guidelines should be in place that encourage employees

> **FAST FACT**
> Did you know that you can now buy paper made from fibers taken from the leaves of coffee plants?

to look for ways to continue using products or find new ways of using products before buying replacements.

10 Use Green Office Supplies

Eco-friendly office supplies benefit the earth, your wallet and your image. As more companies recognize the benefits of selling greener products, you will find that most of your daily office supplies have green counterparts, which you can now add to your shopping list. Some items will be made from recyclable materials and others will be designed to be more energy-efficient. Along with recyclable, environmentally friendly paper products and soy ink for printing, you can purchase earth-friendly, nontoxic, agriculturally based office cleaning products. Two companies, Seventh Generation (**seventh-generation.com**) and Method (**methodhome.com**) are excellent places to look for such products. You'll also find window cleaners that use vinegar and coconut-based soap. For your office kitchen, you can now buy vegetable-based dishwasher detergent and 100 percent recyclable paper towels, or use dishtowels instead. Cups made from a corn-derived resin by Greenware® and Natureworks® can be found at Fabri-Kal (**f-k.com**), among other places.

At the desks, Blue Max lights or similarly made energy-efficient lights are recommended, as are environmentally safe mousepads made from recyclable materials. Check out **bettermousepads.com/recycled** for a variety of eco-friendly possibilities. Nontoxic water-based markers, solar calculators (which have been around for a while), and long-life, refillable pens made from recyclable plastics and other materials are among the other office possibilities.

There are plenty of file folders, hanging folders, and labels made from recycled materials, plus legal trays and in/out boxes made from post-consumer recycled plastic. Even wastepaper baskets can certainly be made from recycled or organic materials. And let's not forget envelopes, which are a major source of paper waste in business. You can go greener here, too. Reusable envelopes can cut your mail costs by 15 percent to 45 percent, by eliminating the need to print, store, handle, insert, track, and include a separate reply envelope. Visit **ecoenvelopes.com** for more information on environmentally friendly envelopes.

The bottom line is, you can go greener in your office environment by letting many small changes add up to an overall large-scale greening of your business. You should get everyone involved in helping find green products you can order for offices or cubicles. Utilize small incentives, such as an afternoon off or a free lunch, for the person who comes up with the most eco-friendly office supplies.

Just by identifying all the typical office supplies, you see where making changes in this category alone will begin to make a positive difference. Once again, the goal is to break old buying habits and instill new ones, which in time will become routine. A couple of places to shop include Twin Supply at **twinsupply.com** and The Green Office at **thegreenoffice.com**.

11 *Use Energy-Efficient Appliances*

Saving energy is one of the cornerstones of becoming a greener business, and can also lead to greater profit margins by lowering your energy expenses. Buying energy-efficient appliances and equipment, as well as being diligent in energy-saving activities, can make a noteworthy impact upon your carbon footprint.

As we are learning from hybrid cars, there are alternative means of energy that can be used to power machines. In addition, there are easy-to-use features that can limit waste, such as those that shift your computer to sleep mode to save energy. It is up to you to research how an appliance or piece of machinery was built to see whether energy efficiency has been a factor before making a purchase.

One way to find the most energy-efficient appliances is by looking for the Energy Star label. Energy Star is a joint program of the U.S. Environmental Protection Agency (EPA) and the U.S. Department of Energy, designed to help individual consumers and businesses find the most energy-efficient products. The program, which began in 1992, initially focused on computers and monitors. Now the program encompasses numerous appliances in all areas of technology as well as energy-efficient buildings, which are recognized as meeting the standards of Energy Star.

The EPA presents an energy performance rating system that has been used by more than 62,000 buildings in the United States. For more information, visit **energystar.gov**.

Along with looking for the most energy-efficient products, it is important to minimize the use of electronics in your office. First, you'll want to understand that computers and other high-tech gadgets have various levels, or "modes," in which they may be utilizing energy, from *active* to *active standby* to *passive standby* to *off*. Read the data sheets or the "specs" and compare energy expenditure at these different modes. If you have a refrigerator and/or dishwasher in your company kitchen or cafeteria, make sure to use energy-saving settings.

Keep in mind that the best way to make sure a device is not draining power when it is not being used is to unplug it. You should also consider using a power strip, which allows you to plug in several items and turn the entire strip off. A surge protector can do the same thing while preventing sudden energy surges from interrupting your work, allowing you time to finish and save your projects.

If you really want to be diligent about your office power usage, buy a power meter or power-use monitor that can apprise you of your power usage, allowing you to gauge how your business is doing and help you decide where you can make changes.

Finally, you may want to look into a high-efficiency power supply. The best of these can improve efficiency by 90 percent. However, others are not really worth the trouble, since they heat up and expend energy in an attempt to help you save energy. To learn more about energy-efficient power supplies, visit **efficientpowersupplies.org**. You can also check out The American Council for an Energy-Efficient Economy at **aceee.org**, where you will find energy efficiency tips.

The bottom line is to purchase appliances and equipment with a greener mindset, which often simply means taking some time to evaluate and compare products and models like a savvy shopper.

FAST FACT

Thanks to Energy Star products, individual consumers and businesses collectively saved $16 billion on their utility bills in 2007.

12 Swith to Energy-Efficient Lighting

While changing light bulbs alone won't qualify you as being a green business, it is certainly a step in the right direction and an easy and cost-effective one to take. It is also one of the many small steps that if practiced universally could make a significant difference. In fact, the International Energy Agency published a report that said a global switch to efficient lighting systems would cut the world's energy cost by 10 percent. It has also been estimated that having just one energy-efficient light bulb in every home in the United States would be equivalent to eliminating the carbon emissions of over one million cars. You can imagine what changing all of the bulbs in each of the millions of small businesses could accomplish.

There are two types of light bulbs that are more energy-efficient than traditional incandescent bulbs: light-emitting diodes (LEDs) and compact flourescent lamps (CFLs). While these bulbs may cost a little more than the traditional bulbs, both will prove cost-effective down the road, because they will last much longer and use significantly less electricity. An LED bulb has a lifespan of 60,000 hours, while a CFL bulb provides 10,000 hours of light—both significantly more than the 1,500 hours of service provided by most incandescent bulbs. LEDs are more durable, although they provide slightly less light. The primary advantage is efficiency. So if your goal is to save energy, LED lights will do the trick. The energy savings comes from the fact that the LED does not have a filament that uses a lot of (wasted) energy as it heats up in order to produce the light. Therefore, the electrical energy used is going directly to generating light, rather than producing heat first and then light.

The CFL bulbs, which Wal-Mart hopes to sell 100 million of, are advantageous over the LED in that the upfront cost is less and they produce a wider range of lighting. LEDs tend to be used more for task lighting. CFLs radiate a different light spectrum than incandescent lamps, but they can usually be used in the same light sockets. Compact fluorescent tubes (CFTs) are the fluorescent versions of CFLs. A CFL or CFT is simply a gas-filled tube with an electronic ballast or control device. Electric current flows through this ballast with the gas inside, creating ultraviolet light, which then powers the phosphor coating in the tube, creating the light you see. This, too, requires less energy than the incandescent light bulb, cutting your energy costs by as much as 66-75 percent if you were to replace all of your lighting with CFLs. It should also be noted that CFLs and LEDs do not emit as much heat as incandescent bulbs, which lowers the amount of cooling your office, retail, or factory space requires during warm weather.

For practical applications, many offices, factories, and retail outlets have LED exit signs designed to be on continually (for safety reasons). LED bulbs are also put to good use where direct lighting is warranted, for display purposes or at work stations. CFTs are more popular for overhead lighting in general work areas. Studies also show that LEDs help people stay alert.

Of course, in addition to using lower-energy lighting options, you can further reduce costs by using light sensors. It's easy to install switchplate occupancy sensors in proper locations that automatically turn lighting off when no one is present and back on when people return. Make sure the sensor is not hidden by furniture, equipment or other items so that it works properly. Of course, common sense helps, too. Turn lights off when they are not in use.

LEDs, CFLs, CFTs, and sensors are produced by well-known manufacturers and are readily available in most stores that sell light bulbs. Read the packaging for installation information. This is a simple and positive step to start on the path to a greener business. Note: Many energy companies also offer rebates for using energy-efficient bulbs. Inquire about rebates from the electricity provider in your area.

13 Upgrade and Maintain Your HVAC System

HVAC, or heating, ventilating, and air conditioning, represents an area of significant energy expenditure. It is also one in which most businesses can make an assessment of their current spending and seek out efficient alternatives to improve their current systems. Of course, some of this will depend on whether you own or rent your business establishment, since climate control systems featuring central air and heating may already be in place and controlled by the landlord and/or building management. In these situations, you may only be able to limit your use and find other means of heating or cooling office space.

If you have control over a central unit or can make recommendations, you will want to look for the zoned approach, where different zones within the building are controlled by individual thermostats. This allows heat or air to be directed as needed, rather than being wasted in empty offices.

For the many businesses that manage their own HVAC systems, the first option is to buy Energy Star heating and cooling equipment, meaning the products have met the strict efficiency guidelines of the United States Environmental Protection Agency and the Department of Energy. Since the HVAC system is typically one of the biggest users of electricity in any business, you can save significant money, up to 20 percent, on your electric bill with a high-efficiency Energy Star heating and cooling system.

For a guide to buying Energy Star HVAC equipment, you can go to **ceedirectory.org**, a website established by the Consortium for Energy Efficiency (CEE) and the Air-Conditioning and Refrigeration Institute (ARI) as part of the Residential Air Conditioner and Heat Pump Initiative and the High-Efficiency Commercial Air Conditioning Initiative.

Keep in mind that when buying an HVAC system, you'll need to check the specs to determine the optimal size for your business. Many companies are using equipment that is too powerful for their spaces, which results in wasted energy.

The second aspect of greener climate control can be achieved through proper maintenance of your current HVAC system, which can keep the system running at peak efficiency and save you money in repairs and on your electric bill. While you can handle some maintenance yourself, you may want to call in an experienced professional twice a year for periodic checkups. You can also buy an annual maintenance contract to ensure that once a year, everything is checked thoroughly.

A maintenance checkup (by a professional contractor or through your maintenance service contract) should:

- Check that all HVAC controls work properly
- Lubricate the motors and any moving parts
- Make sure all electrical connections are tight
- Check to make sure the condensate drain is not blocked up
- Clean evaporator and condenser air conditioning coils
- Clean and adjust blower components
- For heating systems: check all gas or oil connections, gas pressure, burner combustion, and heat exchangers to ensure they're working properly

On your own accord, for better energy efficiency, you can also check the levels of your thermostat on a regular basis, and have a policy stating at what levels it should be set. Also, to maximize your heating or cooling system efficiency, you should seal off vents that are not in work areas. For example, the storage room may need only one or two vents, rather than several. First, seal ducts or vents with duct sealant (mastic) or metal-backed (foil) tape to seal the seams and connections of ducts. Then insulate the ducts, so they do not get too hot or cold. This will eliminate wasted energy in unused offices or other such areas of your business and move the cool or warm air to the necessary areas.

And finally, know when to install a new system, one with a programmable, zoned thermostat. Typically, air conditioners, heating pumps, and furnaces that are over 10 years old are not very energy-efficient by modern standards.

Of course, technology notwithstanding, there's also the common sense element. You don't need to achieve the "meat locker" cooling effect in an office, retail outlet or factory ... not even on the hottest days of summer. Overuse of air conditioning is a major energy waster, and wears out the system much more quickly than if you apply a sensible-use policy. Fans can be an inexpensive, low-power means of cooling an area and minimizing your need for air conditioning. Likewise, closing doors and windows, insulating well, and repairing structural cracks or holes can minimize wasting expensive heat in the winter months. (Find information on insulating your facility in Subsection 14.)

14 *Insulate Your Facility Properly*

A well insulated structure will save on energy expenditures, and thus benefit the environment. While door and window insulation is easier and more obvious, pipe and other insulation is also important and cost-effective. (Find information on door and window insulation in Subsection 15.) In fact, a recent Florida-based study showed that every dollar of energy saved in an HVAC system was the equivalent of $20 of revenue per hospital and $10 per medical office. While savings may not rival those in all offices, it is clear that the less energy you waste, the more money you save.

So what can you do? According to Williamsburg, Virginia-based Ron King, past president of the National Insulation Association and current insulation consultant, there are several places to examine and improve poor insulation, starting with the HVAC. "In many cases the air conditioning ducts are in concealed spaces that are hard to get at. In addition many were installed back in the 1960s and '70s and may be damaged or worn out," explains King.

The next area of concern is hot and cold water pipes. While they may be hard to get to, this can be a major source of wasted energy since temperature-adjusted water travels through them from your water tank. "If the pipes are insulated, the water will get there faster and hot water will remain hotter longer. Again, that deals with energy conservation and also increases comfort," adds King.

The third area to inspect is where the pipes penetrate the wall of the building. Here, too, insulation can prevent unwanted air from getting in or escaping and causing a need for additional heating. Structures often shift slightly over the years, and pipes may have been built with extra air around them, or in some cases, the pipes may have been added to the structure or replaced at a later date. However it happened, if you have gaps where pipes enter your building, the situation needs to be addressed.

Of course, it can be difficult to assess these areas on your own. With that in mind, you should contact an insulation contractor and ask to have an assessment done. One way to find such a contractor is by contacting the Insulation Contractors Association of America (**insulate.org**).

Once you know what needs to be done, you can purchase insulating products and either do the work yourself, if you can easily get to the pipes or ducts, or have it done professionally. For most insulation work, you can use fiberglass, elastic rubber, or types of foams. There are a variety of fiberglass options, including fiberglass pipe covering, fiberglass duct tape, duct liner and wrap, fiberglass pipe and tank insulation. There are also fiberglass batts, rolls, and insulation boards and blankets, which are thermal and acoustical insulation products used for heating and air-conditioning ducts, boiler and stack installations, wall and roof panel systems, tanks, piping, valves, and so on.

For some jobs, you can opt for nontoxic spray forms of insulation, which can reach those hard-to-get-at spaces. Insulation sprays expand to fill the area in which they are sprayed and fill in air gaps tightly. Another possibility is rock wool pipe insulations, which are precision-cut pipe coverings composed of high-density mineral wool. They can perform on pipes that reach temperatures ranging from −120° F to 1200° F. You'll find this type of insulation in high-tempera- ture industrial process power plants as well as commercial hot/cold water systems.

Sealing gaps and cracks with silicone caulk can also be highly effective. Silicone is waterproof and permanently flexible, unlike acrylic caulk, plus it doesn't shrink or crack like acrylic. This alone can save you 10 percent on your energy bills.

Let a professional make the suggestions and then purchase according to your needs. Follow instructions very carefully, making sure all water flow is turned off during installation.

Insulation can be a major energy saver. For example, appliance- grade fiberglass insulation hugging your water heater tank snugly can prevent heat loss and promote energy conservation to the tune of 35 percent of the water heater's total energy usage.

There are many places to buy insulation materials including **buyinsulationproducts.com** and **insulationdepot.com**. You might also want to visit the website of the National Insulation Association for more information at **insulation.org**.

15 Insulate or Replace Windows and Doors

The amount of energy lost through poorly insulated windows, doors, and even skylights can cost you thousands of dollars annu- ally on your energy bills. Heat and cold penetrate single-pane win- dows and air escapes through poor insulation around the frames of windows and doors. A greener work facility should have an inspec- tion of all windows, doors, and skylights to determine what changes may benefit your business and minimize your energy costs and CO_2 emissions.

One option is to insulate existing windows, as long as the actual windows are not permeable to heat. Air coming in around the windows is a less costly problem, since you can use any number of insulation products, including weather stripping, tape, or foam, to seal up openings.

If the windows are older, you may want to consider installing newer, more energy-efficient models. The latest modern windows are scientifically made to achieve a much higher level of energy efficiency than the older, traditional windows found in many buildings older than 20 years. To simplify the terminology, you can focus on a few key factors. For example, there's the U-Factor, which is a measure of the heat that flows through the window. The U-Factor is a function of temperature and is expressed in BTU per square foot/per hour/ per degrees Fahrenheit (BTU/sq. ft./hr./degrees F). The lower the U-Factor, the better the insulation qualities of the window.

An organization called the National Fenestration Ratings Council (NFRC) has developed a rating system based on the U-factor.

- Old metal casement window: 1.3
- Good quality single-pane window: 1.0
- Good single-pane with storm window: 0.6
- Double-pane with low-E glass: 0.4
- Triple-pane with low-E glass: 0.25

The NFRC ratings represent the entire window performance, including frame and spacing material. When shopping for new windows for your company, you'll want them to have a U-Factor of under 1.0. It is easier to make comparisons before looking for new windows by looking at the U-Factor ratings, and NFRC certificates. The amount of air leakage (AL) can also be measured in units or cubic

FAST FACT

According to the United States Department of Energy, the most common sources of air leaks are cracks around windows and doors; gaps along baseboards; mail chutes; cracks in brick, siding, stucco, and foundations; or where external utility lines (phone, cable, electric, and gas) enter the building.

feet, per minute, per square foot, around the frame. A lower air leakage rating—0.30 or under—means the windows are tighter and more energy-efficient with less air seeping into your office or store.

Examine your windows and doors carefully, or look for experienced help to do so. Lack of proper insulation results in millions of dollars spent on unnecessary heating and air conditioning, which is a waste of energy and is certainly not helping the environment.

For more about new windows, visit the National Fenestration Ratings Council at **nfrc.org/about.aspx** or the International Window Film Association at **iwfa.com/industry.htm**.

16 Quick Tip: Buy Air Conditioner and Vent Covers

Along with buying an energy-efficient HVAC system, you'll want to limit heating bills in the colder months. Even when your air conditioner is shut off, it can still cost you money as air filters in through the vents, resulting in the need for more heat in the winter. Conversely, heat escaping through the same vents also requires the need for more energy expenditure. A simple solution is to buy air conditioning covers that conserve energy by reducing heat loss or the intrusion of cold air.

While inexpensive dust covers are one option, you might opt for stronger plastic covers, which are also not very costly considering the money you can save on your energy bill. Known as weatherizing covers, these are made to fit the unit securely and provide added protection to keep the air conditioner in working order for a longer time. The best air conditioner covers are insulated with extra thickness to block cold winds from entering your business or heat from escaping. You'll also find that insulated quilted covers can be very effective.

If you are buying air conditioning covers for existing units, measure very carefully to prevent air leaks around the covers. You'll find some manufacturers have covers for their specific units. In fact, if you are shopping for a new HVAC system, inquire about covers that are designed for the units.

You can also keep cold air from getting into your place of business by purchasing vent covers. Magnetic register sheets are the latest in easy, inexpensive vent covers. For less than $15, and available through most home or office supply stores, they are typically sold in packages of four. Each magnetic cover is 8" x 15.5" and .025" thick. They are easy to cut if you need to, and you can paint them to better match your walls. When you're ready to use your air conditioning, you can leave some of the vent covers in place to direct air accordingly. Make sure to have some vents open, and clean vents periodically.

Once again, like many of the minor recommendations, this practice itself does not make you a green company. It is, however, a small step in the overall greening of your business that saves energy waste while also being cost-efficient.

17 Quick Tip: Pool Your Office Resources

Not everyone needs their own printer, nor does each of a dozen departments typically need their own copier. In a land of overconsumption and overpurchasing, a marvelous way to embark on a greener business culture is to promote the concept of sharing. Network your office printers and look for other office equipment that can be shared within a division or department, or between divisions and departments. The same holds true for office supplies. See if another department has what you need before running out and purchasing another $50 worth of supplies. By doing so, you can minimize the need for shipping and packaging, not to mention save money.

Section 2. Tangibles

Besides saving on energy bills, many small businesses are finding that by minimizing their need for so much "stuff," as George Carlin always called it, they can streamline and fit into smaller spaces, saving on a most significant expense: rent.

You can always expand if your business needs require you to do so, but pooling office equipment and supplies can keep costs down while your business grows.

18 Pool Your Resources with Other Homebased Business Owners

Remember the communes of the 1960s? You may be too young, but the idea has returned, only this time it is for small and home-based businesses.

From shared office co-ops to ordering supplies together in bulk, one way to go greener for home business owners is to pool their resources. Many towns and cities are now offering co-op offices for folks who want to get out of the house and have some office space, but don't need a lot of room. There are numerous advantages, which can even include co-op medical or dental plans, in some cases.

From an environmental and cost perspective, one advantage of shared office space is that heating and cooling one space shared by five or six small business owners is typically less expensive than each person using his or her own home heating or air conditioning. The same holds true for waste, recycling, and so on. Buying supplies as a group is also more likely to be more cost-effective and eco-friendly in such a situation. For example, one person picking up office supplies for four others, or everyone carpooling, is better than each of five people driving to Staples for supplies. Sharing a printer, copier, and other devices is also a plus. Of course, everyone will have to agree to some common group ideas, be like-minded in their concern for the environment, and be flexible for this to work. It all begins with buying into the group mindset and knowing how to work as a team.

If you have a facility in which everyone is part owner, you can even opt to team up to install cooler roofing materials or an alternative energy source, such as solar paneling or a wind turbine, that would cost much more for each individual home business owner.

Even if you are not sharing an office co-op, as a homebased entrepreneur, you can still coordinate with others to buy collectively and order in bulk so that shipping won't mean multiple boxes earmarked for each business. In addition, by establishing a homebased business owners' committee, association, organization, club, or group, depending on how you wish to classify yourselves, you can benefit from recycling equipment and furniture. If, for example, you have two printers and one is sitting idle most of the time, perhaps your neighbor could use it before he or she runs out to buy a new one and yours ends up in a landfill. This holds true for office furniture and a variety of other equipment and supplies.

In the right circumstances, two noncompetitive, businesses that complement one another can save money and paper by doing joint mailings, and teaming up on other forms of co-op marketing and advertising. A shared garden can be a benefit to the community as well as a marvelous way to get to know one another while doing something green.

Pooling resources among homebased business owners is a rather new concept that is starting to catch on as the number of home businesses continues to grow steadily each year. Not unlike the investment clubs of a decade ago, these pools involve teaming up to make money in your business while saving on expenses and helping the environment all at once, not to mention building a sense of camaraderie that can be very welcome since homebased business owners often find themselves cooped up for long hours alone.

19 Create a Green Home Office

Just because you own a homebased business or have a second office at home for your business does not mean you can't go green. The fact that nobody is watching does not minimize the energy you are using or the waste your business is creating.

A homebased green business should be run with the same eco-friendly mindset as any other business. You need to answer the same question: Can your business leave a minimal imprint upon Mother Earth?

One positive thing about running a homebased business is that you should be able to make decisions unilaterally, meaning that if you decide to opt for less A/C and heat, and instead use open windows for cooler air and wear sweaters for warmth in the colder months, you can do so. Step by step, you can think through your office setup as you make changes. For example, you may be working on a desktop PC now, which you can put in sleep mode when you're not at the computer or turn completely off when feasible. However, when you buy a new computer, you can opt to save energy with a notebook. Looking through the suggestions within this book, such as using eco-friendly light bulbs or setting your printer to use both sides, should help you implement small but effective changes.

The key is to look around and determine which areas of your homebased business you can make more energy-efficient. You'll find that some of the simplest steps merely require you to change your habits. For example, get into the habit of printing less and storing more information electronically—be sure to back up important information.

You can also look for environmentally friendly office furnishings. For example, wood can be harvested without destroying trees.

Therefore, furniture made of wood harvested from a sustainable forest or tree farm is an excellent option. Rainforest Alliance certification and FSC certification (Forest Stewardship Council) are indicators of sustainable forestry. There is also furniture made from reclaimed wood that has a Rainforest Alliance Rediscovered Wood certification, meaning wood was used from another source, or recycled. Other groups that certify furnishings are Greenguard and the Business and Institutional Furniture Association (BIFMA). Herman Miller, Haworth, Knoll, and Keilhauer are among the leading manufacturers that make Greenguard-certified furniture.

You'll also find a lot of excellent choices made from bamboo, which also makes excellent flooring. Bamboo is one of the more eco-friendly products now coming into vogue. If you are looking for plastic or metal, again, look for products that are made from post-consumer recycled materials; you'll find plenty. And of course, you'll want to find furnishings that are not coated with toxic chemicals.

Another option is to buy from other business owners, or even homeowners, who are replacing furniture or equipment. My wife's desk at home was in great shape and cost only $10 at a garage sale up the hill from our house. Someone needed to clear out her office, and someone else—and, indirectly, the environment—benefited. Be thrifty, be clever, and seek out good deals at garage sales, yard sales, or going-out-of-business sales. You can get some excellent money-saving deals. As long as you're not meeting clients in your home office, you can focus on comfort, practicality and sustainability over looks. In time, when you are finished with your desk, chair, or computer, look for someone else who is seeking such items and then sell or donate accordingly. Remember that many schools and community and after-school centers need computers.

It's easy to go green at home if you simply set your mind to it and take the extra time to seek out green options. It will save your business money in the end, and you'll feel better about yourself—honest.

20 Quick Tip: Green Up Your Bathrooms

There are several steps you can take to make your bathrooms more green. For starters, you can choose products made from recycled paper or alternative products, rather than those made from trees. Although cloth towels require the energy of washers and dryers, in the long run, they are more environmentally friendly than using paper towels at your business. People tend to take, and waste, more paper towels than they need. Even electric hand dryers are typically a better option, adding very minimally to your electric bill, which isn't a problem if you are using a form of alternative energy.

You'll also want to make sure to have nontoxic, noncorrosive cleaning products. Keep in mind that baking soda mixed with salt and flushed with a container of boiling water can keep your drains free-flowing and prevent buildup. Should you still get a clogged drain, opt for a natural cleaner.

Water is another area where you can be more efficient in bathrooms. You can now install low-flow modern toilets that utilize significantly less water than their more traditional counterparts. Make it clear that people should not dump chemicals into the toilets. In addition, make sure sinks do not drip and there are no leaks from pipes.

Bathrooms are often neglected in the green scheme of office design, which should not be the case. This is an easy part of your business facility to make greener, so make the effort.

If you're working from home, you can also add low-flow showerheads and organic soaps to your own home bathroom.

Natural and Renewable Energy

21 Explore Passive Solar Heating and Cooling

If you've ever sat by the window and felt the warm rays of the sun, you have experienced passive solar heating. Since sunlight is an ongoing source of energy with no switch and no installation, it is considered a passive means of generating energy and heat, meaning no mechanical systems need to be installed.

Yes, you can put up solar panels on your roof and the side of your building, but that is active solar heating, which means taking the concept of utilizing the sun for energy one step further. (Find information on going solar in Subsection 24.) However, for some business owners, installing solar panels does not fit their timeframe or their budget, even though it's relatively inexpensive.

Using passive solar heating and cooling in your work environment is essentially a means of strategically utilizing renewable, natural, environmentally friendly energy instead of more traditional fossil fuel-based energy sources. It can be a simple and very cost-effective manner of greening your environment while also lowering your energy bills in the process.

If you are adding onto your facility or building a new satellite office or retail location, your builders, if they have a green mindset, can utilize architectural techniques to construct your offices for maximize exposure to sunlight. In an existing facility, you may be more limited in your possibilities, but you can still make changes to capitalize on passive solar energy.

"Keeping your place warmer will depend on the season and will be done through the architecture," explains Eric Newman, founder and president of Newman Building Designs in Venice, California. "In a new building, passive solar energy has to do with where you orient your windows and doors. In an existing building, you can add adjustable shading devices to cool the place off during the summer,"

Section 3. Natural and Renewable Energy

adds Newman, recommending an awning or trellis to prevent direct sunlight from coming into your business during the warmer months. "In terms of heating, if you have south-facing windows that let the sun in, you can install the right type of flooring to help you heat the room. You want a thermal mass, which is any material with the capacity to store heat. You can use concrete, stone or anything that actually heats up when the sun hits it," explains Newman.

Skylights are also advantageous for passive cooling and heating, especially operable ones. Opening a skylight allows the heat to rise out of the building, and since the vented air needs to be replaced, it is pulled in from the outside, creating natural convection and making the room cooler.

Part of the strategy in very warm or cool climates is to optimize the passive energy. Depending on the climate, heat can be captured during the day and stored in the thermal mass, then "sealed in the envelope," so to speak, ensuring that closed doors and windows keep the heat in after the sun goes down. Conversely, cooler air can be brought in at night and trapped in the building, where it can help cool off your space during the day. You can also focus attention on cross-ventilation and the direction of prevailing winds, which can be used to bring in cooler air during the nighttime by opening specific windows.

Of course, south-facing windows are a part of the passive solar heating concept that you may or may not have control over, since some landlords frown on tenants adding windows to their buildings. If you are able to build, it is recommended that roughly 8 percent of window to floor area be used on southern walls.

To help any building utilize passive solar energy, it is important to maintain an airtight structure. High-efficiency windows, together with R-2000 levels of insulation and airtight construction, allow passive solar heating to cover a large proportion of heating needs in many locations.

Passive solar energy design can be a very inexpensive means of making a major difference in limiting your greenhouse gas emissions and lowering your energy bills.

Start by looking for a green building consultant or architect, such as Eric Newman (**newmanbuildingdesigns.com**), who can guide you through the possibilities of utilizing passive solar energy for your business.

22 Consider a "Cool" Green Roof

No, we don't mean a hip or trendy roof—a "cool" roof is one that does not accumulate as much heat as many roofs tend to soak up under the sun. On a hot day, it's not unusual for the roof of a building to reach temperatures in the 120 to 150 degrees Fahrenheit range. For those working directly underneath that roof, this may mean significantly higher indoor temperatures and the need for more air conditioning. Therefore, you may consider ways of making your roof greener for the environment and for your own comfort, as well as saving money by lowering your energy expenditure. For example, using materials to make a more reflective roof will result in less heat absorption, resulting in a lower demand for air conditioning. There are paints and synthetics that are also designed to help minimize the level of heat. In addition, proper ceiling insulation can block unwanted heat from getting into your facility. The point is, there are several approaches you can take to a cool a roof that are not particularly costly and can save you a bundle.

To get a good idea of how hot your roof actually gets in warm weather, you might contact the Cool Roof Rating Council. An independent organization established in 1998, the Cool Roof Rating Council can rate the heat level and then help you find the right products to cool your roof. You'll find a great deal of information from their website at **coolroofs.org**.

Another option is to turn your roof green, literally, with plants. Rooftop gardens are not only energy-efficient, but can beautify an otherwise drab exterior. The roof needs to be waterproofed and have prep work done prior to installing planters. Several major companies already have such rooftop gardens in place, including Ford Motor Company's River Rouge Plant in Dearborn, Michigan, featuring 42,000 square meters of plants; Chicago's City Hall building; and Brit's Pub rooftop garden plaza in Minneapolis, where film festivals and concerts are held on nearly 11,000 square feet of topsoil and pea gravel covered with turf.

In New York City, some 35,000 square feet of greenery now sits atop Silvercup Studios, once home to *The Sopranos*, and still a very busy location for movie and TV production. The goal of installing the 1,500 planters, featuring 20 different species of plants, was not only to cool the roof of the TV/film studio, but to absorb rain that caused significant water runoff. A grant from Clean Air Communities, an organization devoted to reducing air pollution and energy consumption in New York City's low-income neighborhoods, helped make this particular roof garden possible. It also indicates that there may be some ways of offsetting your costs by discussing the possibilities with local environmental groups and your local government officials.

Among the more popular plant choices for roof gardens are sedums, in part because they can store water, making them low-maintenance. Mosses and lichens are also possibilities, as are various grasses. You'll want to seek out and talk with a landscape architect who has experience designing roof gardens, especially those that will last without extensive maintenance. A lot will depend on your area's climate. Proper runoff and drainage will also need to be addressed; water from the garden can be collected and reused for cleaning or to water indoor plants. So to cool your office, benefit nature, and add some general environmental beauty, consider a "cool" green roof.

23 Quick Tip: Try Chilled Beams

If you are looking for energy-efficient systems of cooling and ventilation that will reduce your energy bills, chilled beams might be one plausible answer. Of course, you will need to be either building or designing your facility, or adding an extension. Otherwise, it is more difficult, but not impossible, to have such beams installed. Popular in Europe, chilled beams are a newer innovation in American buildings. There are actually two types of chilled beams: passive and active.

The main differences between the two types of beams are the mechanism by which the air flow is promoted and how fresh air is introduced in the occupied space. The passive beams are mounted in or near the ceiling and chilled by an external source, which may be water. Using the laws of physics, natural convection to be precise, the warm air that rises is cooled between coils in the beam system before it returns downward where the cycle begins again. The cost of installing such beams is more than offset by minimizing air cooling energy costs and maintenance to HVAC systems.

An active chilled beam system will utilize an air supply system to generate the cooler air. The air that is supplied then moves through nozzles, inducing extra airflow from the conditioned space through a cooling coil and then down to the conditioned space. Because of the forced convection, active chilled beams typically have cooling densities that double their passive counterparts.

Chilled beams can save energy by maximizing air cooling capacity from either natural resources, such as water used in passive chilled beams, or the air system used in active chilled beams, where ventilation fan energy consumption is reduced. Chilled beams have been used with success in several pharmaceutical projects in the USA and are slowly becoming more popular in green architecture and design.

24 *Go Solar*

Solar panels should be nearly as common on buildings as windows. Unfortunately, they are not. In fact, the percentage of businesses using solar panels is below 5 percent, which is a shame considering that the energy from the sun provides cost savings and does not deplete our energy sources. In addition, the government provides, and will continue to offer, rebates and tax incentives for the use of renewable energy.

Before you can even consider solar energy, you will need to have an assessment or audit to determine if solar energy will work for your business, since some areas get sufficient sunlight while other parts of the country do not.

"We utilize solar maps of the United States which illustrate areas of lower and higher sun ratings," says Roger Strong, a renewable energy consultant for Solar Wind Works in Truckee, California. The ratings are measured in kilowatt hours per meter squared per day, also known as sun hours. "Readings can range from 3 to 7.5; the higher number might be in Arizona or the Mohave Desert," adds Strong, noting that measurements are made before factoring in any shading that might diminish the amount of sunlight. Sometimes trimming branches is in order to minimize shading, which can otherwise diminish the output of solar panels.

Typically, such a reading should be taken into account before a company will install solar panels. The next determination factored into the equation will be how much your business is spending on utilities and what type of rate structure is being used.

"If you are using a high amount of energy, and have a tiered rate structure that has you paying a higher rate based on more usage during certain times of the day when there is considerable sunlight, you may be an ideal candidate for solar energy," explains Strong.

The key is clearly determining how you can best maximize power and minimize your electric bill, since most businesses will not be able to go 100 percent solar.

By using solar power during the higher rate periods of your traditional electric company and then using their service during inexpensive hours, you can set up a system where you pay significantly less for your electric bills while benefiting from renewable energy.

Net metering, now allowed in most states, is the manner in which you gauge how much electricity is being used on the grid, from your electric company, and off the grid, from your solar panels. Power from the solar panels can be used first. Then, the remaining needs are switched to the grid. If there's extra solar power, it goes back to the grid and turns the meter backwards.

So, how much energy will you need? This will be determined by an assessment of your energy use. If, as a small business, you use 1,300 kilowatt hours per month, then, at $9 per watt, your solar system, including installation and equipment, would run $11,700 before rebates and tax credits (9 x 1,300). This will vary depending on your needs.

"Most businesses will remain on the grid, using solar power to cover a substantial amount of their energy needs, but not all. People in remote areas may go completely off the grid, which means running on 100 percent renewable energy. To do this, you will need to have a battery bank to store energy," explains Strong. Such a battery bank can cost $5,000 to $10,000. The solar panels then fill the battery bank with power. "You need either a large enough solar system to match your needs or be able to change your lifestyle to be more energy-efficient. It's either that or have a backup generator ready," adds Strong, who recommends this only for remote locations and/or for someone ready to adjust to a different lifestyle when it comes to energy usage.

Of course, before installing solar panels, the roof should be measured, and a solar pathfinder used to calculate how large a window of incoming sunlight you will have at that location during each month of the year.

Section 3. Natural and Renewable Energy

Since all of the technical work is done by solar professionals, they can ultimately tell you how feasible solar power is for your place of business; then in conjunction with the experts, you can determine how much cost savings you will see on your energy bills as you benefit the environment. And yes, solar panels today are aesthetically pleasing and require very little maintenance once they're installed.

Considering the possibilities and the multiple benefits, we should see far more buildings with solar panels in the future.

25 *Use Wind Turbine Power*

In 1999, a small brewery in Fort Collins, Colorado, New Belgium Brewery, became the largest private consumer of wind-power electricity to date, and the first wind-powered brewery. Today, you'll find an increasing number of wind-turbine-powered businesses in the United States, although far fewer than there should be, considering the tremendous advantages of this low cost means of generating power.

If you are serious about using renewable energy to power your business, or at least have it provide a significant portion of the power used to run your operations, then you should consider this option. Like solar power, wind power will not be effective everywhere. The northern plains, coastal areas, and businesses in and around the Windy City of Chicago are examples of good locations for wind turbine power.

Also, as with solar power, you will need to meet the right conditions. "We look for at least five meters per second for average annual wind speed, which is about 11.2 miles per hour," says Roger Strong of Solar Wind Works in Truckee, California (**solarwindworks.com**). "Average wind speed is very important. If you compare 10 miles per hour to 12 miles per hour you can see a significant difference. The output from wind is measured by the cube of the wind speed, so 10 cubed versus 12 cubed is a 70 percent difference in power," explains Strong, adding that areas with above average wind speed can make exponentially more power, while areas with wind speed below five miles per hour usually cannot justify the cost.

While windmill height should generally be 30 feet higher than the surrounding buildings or trees in a 500-foot radius, there are also small boxes with small propellers that actually fit inside buildings. These small propellers match the aesthetics of some businesses more easily, but they are less effective than the larger windmills. The typical large units are extremely effective and often blend into the landscape in rural locations.

As with solar energy, you'll want to determine how much power can be generated by a wind turbine, and whether or not that will provide sufficient cost savings on your electric bill. Unlike solar energy, wind energy can be generated 24 hours a day. Wind is caused by the uneven heating of the atmosphere by the sun, the irregularities of the earth's surface and the rotation of the earth. Also, like sun, wind is a resource that does not dissipate with use and does not cause any CO_2 emissions. It simply turns the wind turbine, and by way of a generator, produces power.

Typically, wind turbines for a business will cost anywhere from $6,000 to $20,000 installed, depending upon size, application and service agreements with the manufacturer.

Since most small turbines have very few moving parts and do not require any regular maintenance, there is very minimal cost after the initial expense, and the turbines can last 20 years or more. Cost savings will depend largely on the amount of energy necessary to run the business. Typically, the cost of a wind power system will pay for itself after 5 to 10 years when comparing the initial expense to annual energy costs. Also keep in mind that prices for traditional fossil fuel energy will continue to rise, while the cost of wind remains the same.

To start out, you'll want to contact a wind turbine company in your area and have an assessment done to determine whether you have sufficient wind speed to make such an investment worthwhile. An independent energy audit will help as a means of comparing the investment and projected savings to your current energy expenditure. You will also need to check with the local planning board concerning the installation of a wind turbine.

Once upon a time, windmills were a common sight in rural areas here in the United States and around the world. Today, technology has replaced wind power with fuel-burning energy. The problem is that fuel costs money and is destroying the very environment that is our planet. As we are seeing, technology has its downsides, and in going green, you sometimes need to take a step back in time in order to move forward. Stepping back to good old-fashioned wind power can be that major step forward for greening your business, saving money, and making a commitment to the environment, which will be appreciated by future generations.

26 Install Eco-Friendly Flooring

One of the most significant areas of any business facility is the flooring. In busy offices and stores, it requires a durable, long-lasting surface. You can opt for first-class flooring that is also environmentally friendly. While carpeting may be a common choice, only some carpets are made from eco-friendly materials, and many carpets (even those that are eco-friendly) often serve as a home for dust and other particles. Additionally, carpets typically need to be vacuumed, cleaned, and maintained more stringently than other forms of flooring.

"Hardwood or bamboo floors makes strong visual statements and illustrate a commitment to sustainability and health," says Lewis Buchner, CEO of EcoTimber, a national supplier of environmentally sound flooring since 1992. Buchner also points out that woven bamboo, made from long bamboo fibers pressed with resin, can result in a floor that looks like a natural hardwood and is three times stronger than that made from natural bamboo. It also has a very long life cycle. Additionally, EcoTimber sells maple and hickory flooring, all 100 percent FSC-certified. "We believe FSC-certified hardwood sends an important message to the wood products marketplace. There's a preference for FSC, which does more to preserve the land and forest beyond sending a message that people want to buy bamboo," adds Buchner.

Alternatives to wood or carpet include recycled metal tiles, which work well for kitchen areas in particular. Reclaimed wood is also in vogue, from barns or from structural beams and timbers that were once used in old factories. Cork is another flooring alternative, since cork oak trees are not destroyed, but the bark is harvested every nine years. Some of these oaks produce cork for nearly 200 years. Thus, the forest is not damaged or destroyed. Of course, the condition of the wood will factor into its usage, so you will need to carefully review the condition of the product..

Look at **ecotimber.com, ecofriendlyflooring.com** or **corkfloor. com** to get ideas for flooring options.

Ultimately, sustainable, durable flooring can be beneficial to both the environment and to your bottom line, since you hope to get long-lasting use from your flooring.

Water Conservation

27 Start a "Save Water" Program

W asting water has an effect on the environment. It contributes to drying up rivers and streams, which affects fish and wildlife, and it wastes the energy used to pump and filter the water. Of course, the human need for fresh water is also of growing concern, as we continue to use increasing amounts of water because of technology, economic development, and globalization in industrial fields. In fact, we use nearly 50 percent more water today than we did only 25 years ago. If this current rate of water use continues, it is estimated that by 2025 there will be only half the water supply available today for human consumption. There are already over one billion people on the planet who do not have regular access to clean drinking water.

Overlooked in much of the greening process is the need to conserve water. Water-saving programs can be developed in any business, regardless of the industry. However, manufacturing businesses, restaurants, and businesses involved with cleaning, such as car washes, will need to make the greatest efforts because of their extensive water usage.

What can you do to help?

Start by addressing all of your water needs. Then look at where you can start minimizing the use of water. In many instances, you will find you cannot avoid using water, but that you are simply using too much. For example, consider how many companies turn on the sprinklers to water the lawn, only to leave them on for hours when the lawn is more than sufficiently watered. Have you ever seen someone watering the sidewalk outside a retail establishment? Yes, sidewalks should be kept clean, but they should not be turned into small ponds of standing water in the process. The point is, while water is necessary in our daily lives, there's a tremendous amount of water wasted by bad habits and thoughtlessness.

Section 4. Water Conservation

Here are a few water-saving suggestions for businesses in general:

- Don't empty the water cooler or any other water into a drain if you can use that water for another purpose, such as watering plants or cleaning your windows.
- If you have a dishwasher in your company kitchen, wait until it fills up to run it.
- Make sure all pipes in your facility are checked to ensure that you do not have leaks.
- Repair all dripping faucets. You'd be surprised how much money you can save on your water bill by fixing just a couple of leaky faucets.
- Make sure your pipes are insulated so you do not have to wait for warm water.
- Make sure toilet tanks are not leaking.
- Install faucet aerators and low-flow toilets.
- Don't overwater lawns or landscaped areas.
- When building or expanding, work with landscapers who understand the need to conserve water.
- Use plants in your landscaping that are indigenous to your local climate and do not require excessive care.
- Sweep away dirt in front of your facility and water minimally.
- If you have a cooling tower, replace it with a closed-loop version, which can save hundreds of gallons of water daily.
- Seek out steam cleaning when cleaning carpets.
- Support local initiatives that save or reuse water in your community.
- Promote water-saving suggestions to your customers.
- Restaurants can serve water only when requested and ask before refilling glasses.
- Restaurants and others should not use water to thaw out frozen foods.
- When buying new appliances, look for water-efficient models.
- Read your water meter periodically and monitor your bills—if they are going down, then you are taking steps in the right direction.

28 Install a Water Filtration System

Did you know that Americans use over 200 billion gallons of water per day? We also use 10 billion plastic water bottles each year, many of which end up in landfills.

With these numbers in mind, you may want to consider a water filtration system for your place of business. Of course, in this case, being ecologically friendly is only part of the impetus for considering such a system. The other key factor is concern for the health of your employees, as well as yourself.

While water treatment facilities are designed to clean the water we drink, they can only accomplish reasonable levels of what we consider acceptable. In early 2008, it was widely reported that traces of prescription drugs were found in the New York City water supply. Other such stories have not been uncommon. While the health authorities were quoted as saying the levels were not a hazard and within acceptable levels, there is still that nagging concern over what acceptable really means. How many diseases are considered okay for individuals to contract based on these arbitrary standards?

One response is to buy bottled water. However, the critics of bottled water point out that contaminants can form from the plastic and that plastic bottles, as noted above, are ending up in our landfills at an astonishing rate.

So, what kind of water filter might you purchase?

Before exploring some options, you might want to know the basics of how a water filter works. Basically, water passing through a filtration system is cleaned of chemicals and other contaminants in two ways. First, the components of the filtration system literally trap dirt and larger particles. However, chemical contaminants can still filter through. To catch these components, various processes are used to attract the chemicals through magnetic charges. In other cases, such as filtering out chlorine, carbon is included in the filtration system to lure the chlorine away from the water. You can also buy an inline reverse osmosis filtering system if your water test shows sodium, ferrous iron, nitrates, lead, fluoride, or organic contaminants. These systems pull contaminants from the water in a manner similar to the chlorine example cited above, although some waste a lot of water in the process. Look for zero-waste filters that recycle what is typically wasted water with other osmosis systems.

It's advisable, although not essential, that you have your water analyzed to give you an idea of what is coming into your facility. You can then purchase either inexpensive water filters for individual faucets, from a company such as Kohler (**us.kohler.com**), or an inline larger filter that goes into the plumbing system and covers the entire facility, also known as a "whole house" system. Whole house systems can handle the needs of a small business with models such as The Pelican™ Carbon Series PC600 (**pelicanwatertechnologies.com**) or the PureEarth backwashing KDF/GAC (**pure-earth.com**). A good filtration system can reduce or eliminate arsenic(V), barium, chromium, copper, fluoride, lead, radium, and other chemicals found in drinking water.

Obviously, the whole house system is more expensive, running several hundred dollars or more, plus the cost of having it professionally installed. Full facility filtration systems can handle 600,000 or 700,000 gallons of water.

For most small businesses, you can probably manage very well with a filter for your kitchen area faucet(s). Buying a cutoff meter is also a good idea, since it allows you to know when it's time to change the filter.

FAST FACT

Contaminants in our water are part of the ecological fallout that comes from being a highly industrialized nation. In fact, it is estimated that some 75,000 different chemicals are now used regularly in American manufacturing. Many are toxic, and an additional 1,000 contaminants are added each year. Unfortunately, too many of these chemicals find their way into our water supply.

Of course, for many offices, the best option is a bottleless water cooler, which can replace those massive water bottles, while purifying and dispensing clean water. These point-of-use filtered systems also allow you to control water temperature while allowing employees to continue the tradition of discussing sports or the latest *Dancing with the Stars* around the water cooler. Vertex is one place to look for bottleless water coolers (**vertexwater.com**).

Water filters can save your staff money they would have spent on bottled water and ensure that you are contributing to cleaner water and sending less waste to landfills.

27 *Utilize Rainwater*

Want to save energy and cut your water bill? How about utilizing rainwater? Harvesting rainwater, which essentially means collecting and distributing the water for reuse, minimizes the need for power at water treatment facilities and the cost of building and maintaining additional water sources.

Depending on the size of your business and the amount of rainfall in your region, you can determine how much the use of rainwater can serve to minimize your water needs. To most effectively benefit from rainfall, you'll want to have a system where the water collected on the roof is directed into a gutter system where it is then directed as you choose.

"I'm going to use all the rain that comes off of the roof to pass through gutters and drains which will feed into an upper trellis area, which has planters," explains architect Eric Newman of Newman Building Designs, discussing a new commercial project. "The rainwater will come down and flow into these plants. Then once it sinks through these plants, it will be caught again and water the planters on the lower level," adds Newman. Likewise, other water-capture systems can be designed to maximize the amount of water received and then direct water through gutters into large cisterns (water tanks) where it can then be distributed as needed.

Such water can be used for cleaning purposes, used to water indoor plants, or directed for flushing toilets. Roof washers or screens can be installed to remove or capture dirt, leaves, and debris, ensuring clean water. "All we're really doing is taking [the roof] system, which is in place and designed into every building, intercepting the runoff, and diverting it to a storage tank," explains Jerry Yudelson, sustainability director at Interface Engineering Inc. in Portland, Oregon.

Of course, to determine how much rainwater you can actually use, you will have to research average annual rainfall for your region (typically found on the internet or in a local library). Then, you'll want to multiply that by the square footage of the roof. Let's say that the annual rainfall in your area is 15 inches and your roof measures 50 by 80, or 4,000 square feet. Next, take this number (15 x 4,000) and multiply it by .623, which is how many gallons are in an area of one square foot by one inch deep of rainwater. Therefore, you have 15 x 4,000 x .623, which equals 37,380 gallons of water available for use through this system. Of course, you'll want to reduce that number by 10 to 15 percent because you are using an annual rainfall average and because different roofing properties can absorb some of the water before it runs off of the roof. With that in mind, look at metal, tile, or concrete roofing as your best bets for efficient runoff. Gravel roofing is also fairly good.

If at all possible, you will want to use the law of gravity to direct rainwater for your efforts. Of course, if this is not possible, you will need to install pumps to bring water up to a higher location. Sometimes, a closed-looped water collection system can prove effective and provide you with the necessary pressure to raise the water level, but not if you need to go significantly uphill.

Harvesting rainwater is considered a highly responsible means of conservation, and as mentioned earlier, can be cost-effective as long as no one puts a fee on rainwater. While the filtering of rainwater into a plumbing system is typically best left for the building stages of a new facility (since it can be costly), you can certainly consider utilizing a rainwater system for all non-plumbing-related water tasks, which include all cleaning and plant watering.

30 Use Indoor Plants as Natural Air Filters

Not only do they enhance the atmosphere of a sterile office environment and add some color to drab surroundings, but plants can serve a very useful purpose as natural air filters.

These eco-friendly assistants to your green campaign can improve air quality by removing many indoor pollutants, including those from varnish and other laminate finishes, carpet particles and fibers, formaldehyde, and toxins from chemical cleaners and even from high-tech gadgets. In short, it's out with the bad air and in with the good if you utilize plants as natural air filters.

Since not everyone is a whiz with plants, nor will all plants thrive in your office lighting, you'll need to look for plants that require low maintenance and will do well with artificial (low) lighting. From the entrepreneurial standpoint, the key is making a commitment to allowing plants into the office and letting those who have some expertise in the area take the lead in purchasing and caring for these green friends.

Some of the better plant choices for indoor use as office air cleaners include:

- Areca Palm
- Boston Fern
- Cast Iron Plant
- Dracena
- English Ivy
- Golden Pothos
- Hoya

Section 4. Water Conservation

- Peace Lilly
- Philodendron
- Snake Plants
- Spider Plants
- Weeping Fig

These are just a few of many varieties that do well in artificial light and thrive with minimal maintenance. In addition, they'll add warmth and a natural touch to your environment while serving as conversation starters. Typically, if you have your office thermostat set at roughly 65 to 75 degrees, these plants should have no problem. Watering them regularly can be the responsibility of several people, who can utilize collected rainwater channeled through a rain gutter into a cistern, or rain buckets.

The number of plants to buy will be in part based on the décor of your office and the size of your space. According to researchers, you should have at least one potted plant for every 100 square feet of floor space. Therefore, if your office space is 30 by 50 feet, or 1,500 square feet, you should have at least 15 plants. Like many offices, you might opt for different varieties of plants for both aesthetic reasons and because some plants serve different purposes than others. Plants vary in their ability to effectively remove different chemicals and toxins. You'll also discover which ones are easier to maintain and adapt best to your office environment.

FAST FACT

It is not uncommon to have to re-pot a plant, so it fits more comfortably in its container and thrives. A pot made of terra cotta, a type of clay, can be an excellent choice because it helps prevent over watering by absorbing some of the extra water.

Paper and Printing (and Signage)

31 *Start a Paper Waste Prevention Program*

Offices are notorious for wasting huge amounts of paper. Memos alone make up millions of pieces of wasted paper, many of which could be sent as e-mails or combined into one larger company memo. While recycling paper is a marvelous idea, it is important to stop wasting paper. Why, you might ask? Because, along with the concerns about diminishing forests, paper requires a considerable amount of energy to produce. It takes the equivalent of nearly 17 watt-hours (Wh) of electricity to make a single sheet of paper from wood (and about 12 Wh for 100 percent recycled paper). Consider the amount of energy expended by the average office worker who uses 10,000 sheets of paper per year. In fact, if you consider that paper usage in the United States stands at four million tons of copy paper (or 27 pounds per person) the cost is over $4 billion per year to buy paper, not including cardboard.

What all of this means is that a waste paper prevention program can save both paper and energy use in a significant way. To begin, you will want to get everyone onboard through e-mail memos explaining your paper-waste prevention policies and possibly reward incentives for reaching specific goals. One of the simplest and most underutilized means of conserving paper is using both sides of a sheet as often as possible. Two-sided printing should become standard protocol, especially for in-house materials. You can set your photocopiers and printers to print on both sides by default. In addition, you can take a significant step toward a paperless office by encouraging electronic memos, limited printing and copying, and posting manuals, policies, and other documents online, or allowing employees to access PDFs via the company intranet at their leisure.

To encourage participation, you can utilize the team approach, and have everyone add to an online list of ways and means to save

Section 5. Paper and Printing (and Signage)

paper. While there will always be a need for some hard copies in any office, such as legal documents, contracts, and tax information, wherever paper use can be limited should be included on the list. Also, if you scan material into a computer, do not toss the paper. You can use the back, if it is blank, for note taking. You can also try to get everyone into the habit of taking notes at meetings on the back of printed pages that come into the office as junk mail.

Other simple tips include photocopying both pages in a book on one sheet of paper, perhaps legal size, then also using the back. For message and note taking, you can also use any of the handheld electronic products such as Blackberrys, organizers, or even some cell phones. A website such as **palm.com/us** is a good place to start looking at such devices.

Another way to go greener with paper is to shop with an environmental mindset. This means purchasing paper with a high percentage of post-consumer recycled content instead of paper from 100 percent virgin pulp. Often, you'll see "recycled" on the label, but ask whether that means the paper is made from post-consumer recycled content; often it does not. If that's your only choice, it's still better than nonrecycled paper. Look for at least 30 percent recycled content in uncoated paper and 10 percent in coated stock. You also want to buy processed, chlorine-free paper. Once you get into the habit of purchasing more environmentally sound paper, spread the word by mentioning on your printed documents that your business uses eco-friendly paper.

REUSE IT

Shred and reuse unwanted paper. Rather than tossing old documents, unwanted catalogs, or junk mail in the trash, you can buy an inexpensive shredder, and shred paper to use as packing material in shipments.

The truth is that once an office gets out of the disposable paper mindset and begins to recognize the value of paper conservation, habits will change, and you and your staff will become more aware of additional ways to save paper. It's all a matter of embracing the mindset.

32 *Switch to Green Printing*

From catalogs, books, manuals, brochures, and promotional materials to packing slips and receipts, businesses remain quite immersed in printed papers, even in this so-called paperless world.

While it may not seem like a major blot on the environment, the use of ink and printed matter in businesses is one of the most significant contributors to global warming and the environmental damage to our planet. The paper-pulp industry is the third largest contributor of pollution in the industrialized world, and the use of water in the paper-making process makes the industry the largest polluter of water. Add to that the destruction of forests, the subsequent effect on wildlife, and the various chemicals in ink and paper manufacturing, and you have several good reasons to rethink how you use printed matter.

Fortunately, there are fairly simple ways to make the transition to greener printing. Once again, it requires a little effort on your part to instill the green printing mindset in your work environment.

Your obvious first step is to use only recyclable paper for all printing. Amazingly, only about 10 percent of paper used in business is recyclable, despite the awareness of the need to save trees and use recycled paper. Therefore, you cannot assume that commercial printers are using recycled paper. You should also know that there are different degrees of recycled paper. You want to use, or patronize printers who use, no less than 50 percent post-consumer content.

Next, you should know a little about the use of chlorine and its derivatives as they pertain to papermaking. For years, paper mills have used chlorine gas in papermaking, which causes the formation of dioxins and other highly toxic waste materials. Today, however, you can find processed chlorine-free (PCF) paper, which is made without the use of chlorine or chlorine derivatives. Again, you should also be seeking post-consumer recycled, rather than virgin paper.

Section 5. Paper and Printing (and Signage)

The next step is to find ink that is not petroleum-based and environmentally harmful. The commonly used alternatives today are soy-based ink or other vegetable-based inks, which are less harmful to the environment than their petroleum-based counterparts. These products have low levels of volatile organic compounds (VOC), such as 5 to 15 or 20 percent, while other commercial inks measure over 30 percent. Besides being better for the environment, soy-based ink is easier to recycle on paper and can be better for the life of your printer. Additionally, it will be cost-effective over time. You'll also find vinegar ink and inks made from castor, canola, linseed, and safflower. While soy and other vegetable inks are often blended with pigment or waxes, and are not 100 percent biodegradable, they are a major step forward from ink that relies on petroleum.

Of course, one of the biggest sources of wasted energy and paper is the vast amount of overruns found in most businesses. We have 200 employees, so we print 300 copies. We need to mail out 10,000 fliers, so let's print 15,000. More than 35 percent of the printed matter in business today ends up being disposed of without even being distributed. Making realistic estimates of the amount of printed matter necessary is another factor in minimizing waste. Therefore, you need to assess your printing needs and determine where you can make cuts. Which printed materials can be moved to e-mails, PDF files, and online documents? When printing, where can you eliminate pages? Can you maintain control over your inventory, ordering only the quantities of paper and ink you need? Are you reusing and recycling unused inks and paper? Establishing greener printing practices means taking all of these things into account. In the end, green printing can be a major step into a greener overall business environment.

And if you are using outside printers, look for those with green printing policies, which include using soy or vegetable-based inks, paper made from a high percentage of post-consumer recycled fiber, and alcohol-free printing.

Also, finding printers that use computerized pre-press systems eliminates the need for additional chemical use.

"The trend today is moving heavily to soy-based ink and recyclable paper. It's no longer the exception, but what the majority of customers want," says Brooklyn-based printer Avery Marder of Trademark Graphics.

For more on green printing, you can check out Green Printer at **greenprinter.com** or go to Quad Graphics at **qg.com**.

SMALLER CARDS

For your own personal signs or your business cards, you can save plenty of paper by opting for smaller cards. Another advantage of the smaller business card: people will take notice of them. And you can use soy-based ink to have them created just for you.

33 *Use Greener Signage*

Glo Brite® and Eco Exit™ are two of the newest signs created by Jessup Manufacturing Company in an effort to help companies save energy. The latest in safety signs consume no energy and need no maintenance. You can check out their signs at **jessupmfg.com**, and consider other ways in which you can create and utilize greener signs. Photoluminescent signs can save a business hundreds of dollars in energy costs and reduce air pollution significantly, when compared with more commonly used incandescent signs. LED Exit signs are another alternative means of reducing your energy use and lowering your carbon footprint.

For in-office signage, you can consider poster boards made from recycled materials, particularly post-consumer recycled materials. Additionally, redesigning and reusing older signs can cut down on expenses and the need to purchase new signage. Many in-store and in-office signs can be reused or purchased at closeouts from other stores, thus recycling the product.

Section 5. Paper and Printing (and Signage)

As for the outdoor signage that brings people into your establishment, vinyl signs are very popular, but not eco-friendly. Therefore, if you can create a sign using re-cycled wood and nontoxic paints, or recyclable plastics, you can take a step in the right direction. Remember, vinyl signs have only become popular in recent years, meaning that ingenuity was long a part of the sign-making process in the pre-vinyl days.

Greener Packaging, Design, and Packing

34 *Implement Sustainable Packaging Policies*

Y ou've heard the term, but what exactly is sustainable packaging, and how can you make it an integral part of your business? Sustainable packaging is designed to minimize the natural resources and energy wasted in packaging, which weighs in at more than 75 million tons annually, with less than half being recycled.

The idea of sustainable packaging is to make closing the loop your goal: that is, in the life cycle of the package, the products should begin in nature and after they've served their purpose, they should end in nature. Materials used for sustainable packaging need to be biodegradable, made from recyclable and reusable materials, and created through eco-friendly methods.

Using recycled materials presents an opportunity to recover valuable raw materials, thereby allowing you to create economic value by eliminating the basic extraction and processing steps. Still, there is so much more that can be done to increase sustainability.

The first step toward implementing sustainable packaging policies is to assess your packaging needs and review the current life-cycle chain. From where are you getting your packaging materials? What actual materials are being used? What is the shipping process? What is the process of creating packages?

Next, you'll want to start exploring where you can make changes. Can you maximize the use of renewable/recycled material? Can you eliminate energy-using steps in the process? Is your packaging physically designed to optimize materials and minimize energy use?

Beginning the journey to sustainable packaging starts at the top of the organization with a commitment to long-term change. It requires that all departments are on the same page and have the same economic, social, and environmental concerns and commitment to making the necessary changes. Some changes are more practical, such as utilizing biodegradable rather than petroleum-based plastics. Other solutions may include using materials with recyclable natural fibers or corrugated cardboard. Possibilities need to be researched and explored, starting with the manufacturers and moving through the chain to the customer.

Retailers are becoming increasingly conscious of the packaging they receive and market to their customers. Wal-Mart's packaging scorecard, which was officially implemented in early 2008, rates the manufacturers and suppliers on the sustainability of their packaging. They look at the sustainability goals of reducing waste, using renewable energy, and selling sustainable products. Wal-Mart and other retailers then pass that sustainability on to consumers.

In an age of disposable products, from cameras to contact lenses, the key is to stop and take a conscious look at what is being thrown away and where it goes once discarded. While it won't work with contact lenses, in Canada, the beer industry has instituted and maintained a closed loop return system for beer containers. In short, customers reuse the same bottles as many as 15 times before the bottles are melted and recycled into new bottles. Thus far, this system is working very well in Canada, with over 90 percent of bottles sold being reused and refilled by customers.

Along with considering the ramifications of packaging and its transportation, it is worthwhile to determine if reuse is a possibility. With some products, such as the Canadian beer bottles, it can work well. The result is less energy used in bottle manufacturing and even less recycling, which minimizes subsequent pollution. Of course, as with everything else, the practical application and process of reusing a product must be considered. Certainly, many types of packaging can be reused and businesses must encourage such reuse.

The Sustainable Packaging Coalition envisions a world where all packaging is:

○ Sourced responsibly
○ Designed to be effective and safe throughout its life cycle

- Meets market criteria for performance and cost
- Made with renewable energy
- Recycled efficiently to provide a valuable resource for subsequent generations

The Coalition's mission is to advocate and communicate a positive, robust environmental vision for packaging and to support innovative, functional packaging materials and systems that promote economic and environmental health through supply chain collaboration. For more on the Sustainable Packaging Coalition, go to **sustainablepackaging.org**.

> **FAST FACT**
> Did you know that $1 out of every $11 that Americans spend on food goes to packaging?

For your purposes, start by getting everyone onboard to make sustainable packaging a goal of your company, with incentives for the best, most feasible ideas.

35 *Minimize and Redesign Your Packaging*

You may have noticed the redesign of soda and water bottles. For example, Pepsi has minimized the plastic in their latest bottles and Coca-Cola has been changing the design of Dasani water bottles and cutting plastic usage by 7 percent simply by tweaking the bottle design. Poland Spring's Eco-Shape™ bottle is also specifically designed to use less plastic. These are a few of the many new package designs produced by companies that are working hard to become more sustainable.

Procter & Gamble, for example, introduced rigid tubes for Crest toothpaste that can be shipped and displayed on shelves without boxes. Meanwhile, Aveda, a beauty products company, is working on a men's care line that is packaged in bottles made of 95 percent recycled materials. And the folks at Estee Lauder spent over a year working with aluminum smelters to create a new tube design made with 80 percent recycled aluminum.

These types of packaging changes are not only reserved for the major corporations. Green Mountain Coffee Roasters worked in conjunction with International Paper to create an all-natural paper hot beverage cup, which they called the ecotainer™. Following Sustainable Forestry Initiative (SFI) guidelines for management and harvesting the trees used to make the paper for the cups, the ecotainers come from waste recovery. In the packaging industry, Connecticut-based Curtis Packaging also worked hard to create environmentally sound packaging products for their primarily high-end clients. Instead of using foils, which are commonly used but not recyclable, Curtis came out with a product called Curt Chrome, which is an environmentally-friendly alternative to foil. It uses metallic-based ink and is 100 percent recyclable. RPC Cresstale, part of the RPC Group in Europe, launched biodegradable lipstick and compact packaging made from PHA, a polymer made of organic sugars and oils. They have plans to come out with a whole spectrum of color cosmetic products to meet rising demand for recyclable products and packaging.

The point is, environmentally sustainable packaging is not only in vogue, but it is the future of packaging. With that in mind, Kraft Foods developed what they call the Eco-Toolbox to assist packaging designers. The Eco-Toolbox compares material type, material weight, recycled content, recyclable materials, and other key factors when considering the increased sustainability of a package. You too, can develop your own "toolbox" or at least a list of criteria to look at when designing your company's packaging.

First, you want to examine what your products require for safe shipment to another location and possible shelf life, depending on the product. Of course, you will also want to consider the necessary weight, temperature, and size necessary for packaging your products.

Often a packaging redesign can simply minimize the amount of material used. Many products use far more packaging materials than necessary. Excessive interior packaging materials are common and easily reduced or eliminated.

You will want to consider the recyclable and biodegradable material alternatives, from biodegradable plastics or recyclable cardboard to materials made from natural fibers and/or other recycled items.

Your goal is to design safe, cost-effective packaging that is sustainable, recyclable, reusable, or refillable by the consumer or retailer and strong enough to withstand shipping. Of course, in most cases, you are not inventing the wheel and can explore the products already making their way to the shelves, such as those mentioned above, to see what materials are being used effectively. The initial exploration, evaluation, design, and creation stages will take some time and cost money. However, the right solution will prove extremely cost-effective in the long run and can boost your profile thanks to the positive responses you will receive from customers. Numerous businesses have used promotional campaigns featuring their new sustainable packaging to generate a buzz, ultimately increasing sales among eco-conscious consumers while spreading the word to other businesses that eco-packaging is a distinct possibility.

36 Use Eco-Friendly Packaging Labels

Each year, billions of dollars' worth of energy is wasted on product labels. The process of printing labels, cutting them out, and applying a glue of some type wastes acres of materials and uses millions of gallons of petroleum.

Of course, there are alternatives. Environmentally-friendly Earth-First® PLA label materials are made from corn, a renewable resource. This allows for more environmentally friendly labels with scratch-resistant coating that look just as good as their petroleum-based counterparts.

Section 6. Greener Packaging, Design, and Packing

A company in Farmingdale, New York, Seal-It, Inc., is now offering the latest in the shrink-film label market. The labels are made from a film based on renewable resources that has proven to be competitive in terms of cost with most traditional petroleum-based films.

There are plenty of other options made from recyclable materials or corn-based materials that you can utilize when designing company product labels. Woven tags can also be used for fabrics.

Another option that you'll see on Heineken beer bottles is screen printing the label right on the bottle, which neatly avoids the use of additional materials for labeling. Far too few products use this process, but having your name, logo, or both printed directly on the bottle or container cuts out the labeling process entirely. Plastic bottles, including those for many hair products, already utilize this concept; however, many other industries have been slow to adapt. While costs may be higher, depending on volume, size of packaging, and other considerations, you will be forging your way into greener territory.

Of course, bottles without labels can be reusable, such as the Swiss-designed SIGG lifestyle bottles (**mysigg.com**). Made from a single piece of aluminum, the bottles are crack-resistant and completely reusable and recyclable. Reusable products, as some Canadian beer companies have seen, can be a cost-saver in the long run.

While screen printing right on the packaging is one option, it can take time since it is a slower process. With that in mind, you might consider heat-shrink wrap labels, which are less expensive than screen printing and can be completely earth-friendly.

Seal-It Inc. offers heat-shrink sleeve labels in 10 colors that are all natural, corn-based, and 100 percent annually renewable. See **sealitinc.com** for more information.

While new technologies continue to explore eco-friendly options, eco-friendly shrink wrap and screen printing are certainly options worth exploring for your product labels and logos.

37 *Use Eco-Friendly Packing Materials*

While you're evaluating product packaging, you will want to consider the packing materials you use to ship products. These too can be eco-friendly. Sure, bubble wrap is fun, but since it's made from polyethylene, the popping plastic is not at all good for the environment. And those Styrofoam peanuts you see pouring out of boxes aren't much better. Both of these products and similar items are landfill fodder. Therefore, if these are among your commonly used packing materials, you have another area in which you can make significant changes to make your business greener.

While manufacturing companies will need to find sustainable packaging solutions on a large scale, many small businesses need to simply find ways to pack shipments on a day-to-day basis for their customers. You can seek out alternative packing materials and provide a little promotional message that explains your sustainable goal to your customers to help spread the word about better packing practices.

Here are some packing ideas you can implement. Most products, even those that are fragile, do not require the sheer volume of packing materials often found in shipped boxes, nor do they need to be wrapped in an abundance of materials. We habitually overpackage products, and habits can easily be replaced with cheaper, environmentally friendly alternatives. For the peanut lovers out there, biodegradable packing peanuts are available, made from grain sorghum and cornstarch. Besides being 100 percent biodegradable, they are static-free and not affected by oil prices. There are various brands available, including Puffy Stuff, which is quite durable and cost-effective. See **puffystufftn.com**.

Another packing option is fabricated soft foam that comes in rolls, which is also environmentally friendly and made from high-grade cornstarch and soybean oil. This foam can be used for cushioning technology products, electronic equipment, or lightweight products. Green Cell from KTM Industries at **greencellfoam.com** is an example of this particular product.

For oddly-shaped and/or fragile items, you might start using Cushion Cubes from UFP Technologies,Inc. Made from 100 percent recycled paper fibers and water, the cubes can be used to cushion packed items, while serving as an alternative to packing peanuts or other chemically made products. For more information visit **cushioncube.com**.

For some items, you can use pea straw, which has good cushioning properties. Recipients can even plant your packaging materials—talk about organic! If you can resist the urge to eat your packaging, you can use popcorn, which has become a popular alternative packing material. The popcorn is packed in recyclable paper bags to prevent it from breaking into smaller pieces. Thin shredded wood shavings, known as excelsior, are also a good natural packing material, as is the old standard: rolled up newspaper. You can also shred cardboard boxes and use the rolled-up strips for packing.

The bottom line is that if you find a natural packing material that can be recycled, reused, or returned to the earth, you are becoming greener.

Promote the concept of sustainable packing and it will catch on. Remember, part of bubble wrap's initial appeal was that it was unusual. If new, sustainable packaging is marketed creatively, there's no reason it can't enjoy similar success.

38 Consider Reusable Bags Over Plastic or Paper

We've all been faced with the question: Paper or plastic? Whether we're in a retail business that supplies bags to customers or standing in line at the grocery store, we're put in the position of needing to choose. If we're concerned with making green choices, we want to choose wisely. While a number of companies have been promoting paper over non-biodegradable plastic bags, there are increasing objections to this stance that are worth exploring.

First, let's consider some numbers. According to the Environmental Protection Agency, the United States consumes over 380 billion plastic bags, sacks, and wraps each year, throwing out at least 100 billion polyethylene plastic bags, or more than 95 percent of the bags, which means less than 5 percent are recycled.

The alternative, paper bags, are not as environmentally-friendly as one might think. After all, those 10 billion paper bags used every year take more than one billion trees to make. In fact, according to the EPA, producing paper bags generates 70 percent more emissions, and 50 times more water pollutants than producing plastic bags. Even paper bags made from 100 percent recycled fiber use more fossil fuels in their production than plastic bags.

Of course, the argument is made that paper bags can be recycled. The argument for plastic bags is that they too can be recycled or reused as lunch bags, for garbage, etc. While there are plenty of arguments for either side being more environmentally friendly, the truth is that discarded bags, paper or plastic, are never a boon for ecology. The processes of making both paper and plastic bags are detrimental to the environment. In fact, some states, cities, and municipalities are in the process of banning them altogether. San Francisco, for example, as of late 2007, allows grocery stores to use

Section 6. Greener Packaging, Design, and Packing

plastic bags made from compostable material. Several countries in Europe, as well as China, also have bans or restrictions to limit plastic bags in place.

In Ireland, 1.2 billion plastic bags were used annually as of 2001. The following year, the government created a plastic bag consumption tax, meaning consumers would have to pay 15 cents per bag. By the end of 2002, plastic bag consumption was down by nearly 90 percent. At some point, the United States government will begin taking environmental problems more seriously and follow suit. Restrictive taxes could apply, not only to plastic bags, but to paper bags as well.

So, what can you do? As a retailer, you can help change the habits of your customers. For starters, you can utilize plastic bags that are compostable or paper bags that are made largely from post-consumer paper. However, you can go one step further and promote reusable cloth or canvas bags for carry-out items. If you can afford to give them away, do it! If not, sell them at a nominal cost. Customers can then bring them back each time they shop at your store, and as a bonus receive a coupon, discount, or some other incentive to make reusing bags an ongoing part of their shopping ritual.

You can (and should) promote your business on the bag with the message that this is a reusable bag. You can even check out **reusablebags.com** to get an idea of what you can offer your customers. Yes, there will be an initial cost, but, in the long run, once you have armed your customers with bags, you will spend far less buying paper or plastic bags in bulk.

Another option, if you own a retail store in a mall, is to team up with other store owners and buy bags together with the names of several stores or the name of the mall, therefore making it the bag for shopping at a variety of stores.

The point is, as a retail store owner, one of the most obvious ways to go green is to significantly decrease the use of disposable bags. Any environmentally friendly business owner should try to instill in his or her employees the understanding that disposable bags are unnecessary. Give out reusable bags for bringing lunch, going on lunchtime shopping trips, or other uses.

Section 6. Greener Packaging, Design, and Packing

Don't get caught up in the paper or plastic debate. Choose neither in your effort to make a greener business and influence your employees and customers.

Technology

39 Switch to Energy-Efficient Computer Use

Computers are a major part of almost all industries, and while they have changed the face of modern business, they have also changed the face of the environment by using, and wasting, their fair share of energy. In fact, it is estimated that most computers use roughly half of the power they receive. With that in mind, you want to start promoting greener computer use in your company. Also, by properly managing usage, you can increase the lifetime effectiveness of your computers.

While they were a trendy way of saving your monitor's screen several years ago, screensavers are no longer in vogue, as they actually use up a lot more energy from the CPU: plus, the latest monitors no longer require the use of screensavers. One very simple alternative that is better for your system and the environment, is to get into the habit of switching your computer to sleep mode for any periods of inactivity. In fact, you can have your computer switch to sleep mode automatically after 10 or 15 minutes, if you will be away from it for any length of time. The system then "awakens" with a touch of a key or the mouse. Instructions for enabling power management vary by operating system. You may need to be "off-network" to use sleep mode effectively. Keep in mind that by setting the time of inactivity at which your computer will go into sleep mode at a lower number—after 10 minutes, rather than 20—you save more energy.

Of course, you can also make sure that all business computers are shut off overnight, including the monitors, which is an obvious way to save energy. The same goes for other peripherals, such as printers and scanners. You might also use a smart power switch that shuts off all peripherals automatically when the main CPU is switched off.

Section 7. Technology

Excessive graphics are also a major waste of energy, as much as 100 watts. You do not need high-performance graphics cards for many types of business operations, particularly those dealing with finance, schedules, and word processing. Choose a graphics card that meets your needs, or simply do not upgrade for flashier graphics if they are not germane to your business needs.

You'll also find that numerous programs are running on your computer at one time, slowing down your system and utilizing more energy. Do you really need all of the programs that are currently on your computer? Also, check your settings. For example, you may be able to lower the brightness setting on your monitor. And finally, opting for laptops over desktops can also increase energy savings, as they use less power.

These are just some ways in which to utilize your computer in a more energy-efficient manner. Then, once it's time to buy replacement computers, you'll want to find a place to donate your current computer equipment so it avoids becoming part of the mass of landfill.

Smarter computing is very simple when it comes to going green. In fact, in some offices, the idea of flex schedules allows for computer sharing so that fewer computers are on at all times.

40 When Buying New Computers, Buy Greener Models

Let's face it, the world of technology—computers in particular—has come at us over the past 20 years at a rampant pace, with new models making your computer outmoded minutes after it's removed from the box. The problem, however, is that in our haste to make faster, lightweight, memory-enhanced, compact, powerful, state-of-the-art computers with features galore, Mother Earth has taken a backseat to motherboards. In the past few years, however, after dazzling us with sharper graphics and printers that spew out reams of unnecessary pages at faster speeds and in brilliant colors, the computer industry has begun to hear rumblings about their products from a more environmentally savvy buying market. Yes, many of us have rolled back in our ergonomically designed computer chairs and realized that our PCs, laptops, and notebook buddies were not compatible with our greener mindset.

As a result, and in response to the commotion, greener PCs have finally begun to emerge. Therefore, when it is time to purchase those new office or business computers and peripherals, you can think green. Today's newer models are more environmentally efficient and use lead-free components, while avoiding energy-wasting power supplies and souped-up graphics cards. They also come with LCD monitors, which use less power than their CRT counterparts.

Along with environmentally friendlier computer usage (discussed in Subsection 39), you can save energy and money by purchasing from the new line of greener computer equipment.

The first step you can take when embarking on your search is to look for Energy Star-compliant computers and monitors. According to Energy Star, their latest computer requirements (as of late 2007) are expected to save consumers and businesses more than $1.8 billion in energy costs over the next five years and prevent greenhouse gas emissions equal to the annual emissions of 2.7 million vehicles. These computers have been tested and shown to use less energy while the machine is idle. According to the Natural Resources Defense Council, idling represents 69 to 97 percent of total annual energy use, even if power management is enabled. Being idle, by the way, does not mean the computer is not being used. It means that no continuous program is being used. Playing music or having an active USB device means that something is actively running, whereas data entry tasks on a spreadsheet or keying in a word processing program are tasks that don't activate the system until the documents are saved. When no program is active, most operating systems today will put the computer into a sleep or standby (idle) mode to save power during long periods of inactivity. Obviously, you can check to make sure the operating system in the model you

Section 7. Technology

choose has this feature, which has become fairly standard.

Since most desktops use roughly 100 watts and up for high-powered games (which should not be allowed in the workplace, anyway), you want to look for the new breed of eco-friendly computers
that use less than 75 watts while in use, less than 50 watts while
idle, and 4 watts in sleep mode. When looking at laptops, you should
look for models that use less than 35 watts when in use, less than 15
watts while idle, and 2 watts when in sleep mode. Once upon a
time, your PC would run on full power at all times. Today, you can
and should minimize power as much as possible when you are not
using your computer, and remember screen savers are power eaters.

Much of what you will need to know can be answered by computer experts at leading stores as well as by manufacturers. Reading
the latest computer magazines, including *Computerworld* and *PC
World*, can also help you find answers. Here are some features you
may want to research or ask about:

- Variable CPU fans with heat sinks can limit heat from the CPU
  and keep your power supply cooler.
- Lead-free circuitry and hard drives are available from Sam-
  sung, Seagate, and other manufacturers.
- Lead-free DVD/CD drives are also available.

You can also monitor your system's power with the right software
program.

SURVEYOR, made by Verdiem, is a user-friendly software feature that lets you gauge and manage the amount of energy used by
your computer network or system In fact, SURVEYOR can reduce
your kilowatt-hours (kWh) from 300 to 100 for each PC in your company, giving you major cost savings. You can also get Energy Star-
administered software tools distributed free from the EPA: EZ Save.
EZ Group Policy Object (GPO) and EZ Wizard are all monitoring
and power management tools available from the EPA. Visit
energystar.gov.

Keep in mind that some greener computers sacrifice performance
in other areas. If these are minimal sacrifices or areas in which you

do not need top-of-the-line features, then you will be just fine. For example, if the graphics will not play the latest in high-graphic games, you probably won't care since these are your business computers—unless of course, your business is reviewing computer games.

Review computers by looking at greener features, such as faster cooling systems, power savings, and so on. Then see if your needs can be met by these new, environmentally friendlier models.

COMPUTER SHOPPING: SOME GREEN FAVORITES

If you like green apples, MacBook Air may be for you. Along with a fully recyclable aluminum case and a mercury free LCD display with arsenic-free glass, the lightweight Energy Star-compliant computer has 50 percent less packaging than the previous MacBooks. You'll also want to check out the new MacBook Paper, which may be even greener. Although they won't save you on green from your wallet, as they are pricier than other lightweight laptops, the green Macs are top-of-the-line models.

Some other leading models you may want to consider include:

- Zonbu Desktop Mini, the Zonbu notebook and the Everex gPC VIA (E80-TC2502), which is similar to the Zonbu desktop, but comes with an 80 GB hard drive, CD-RW/DVD, speakers and similar software, without any subscription, for only $200, you only have to add a monitor.
- From Dell, the Ortiplex 755 and the Latitude D630
- From Toshiba, the Tecra A9-S9013
- From Leventro, the Think Centre a61e
- From Apple, the Mac mini, along with those mentioned above
- From Fujitsu, a higher-end model called the Lifebook S6510

From HP Compaq you'll find the HP Compaq dc7800 and the barebones model dc5800. Energy-efficient hardware as well as software in these Energy Star-compliant computers results in faster boot-ups, as-needed power consumption, and timely auto shutdowns. They also reduce cooling energy by 15-30 percent.

Of course, by the time you read this, the latest in green computers may have been replaced by newer greener computers. Nonetheless, keep these in mind and don't get lured into purchasing additional features that require more energy expenditure and are unnecessary for your needs.

41 Start a Company-Wide Computer/Cartridge E-Cycling Program

What is e-cycling? It is recycling of electronic equipment, from computers to cell phones. Electronic waste is the fastest-growing waste concern worldwide. It is one of the most significant concerns of ecologists and should be a major concern to everyone who cares about the health and welfare of our planet for future generations. Unfortunately, that is not the case. There are towns in various parts of the world are primarily known for e-waste accumulation, which fuels their meager economic growth while raising pollution to unhealthy levels. This is in large part due to the fact that, of the millions of printer cartridges purchased every year in the United States alone, less than 7 percent are recycled. Most of us are guilty of taking the cartridge and, in an attempt to stay clean, dumping it in the trash, when it could just as easily be put in a bin that is marked for recycling. It's all a matter of taking the extra time to find a cartridge recycling program; if you do a search on the topic, you'll find several. If you consider that the plastics used in printer cartridges can take literally hundreds of years to decompose, and that the average small business may use as many as 100 cartridges a year, you'll have a better idea of how important it is to keep cartridges from adding to the vast amount of landfill already accumulating.

Computers are another cause of waste, with most users, including businesses, replacing computers once every three years on average. Unlike a cartridge, however, a used computer may still have plenty of life left in it and can be a tax deduction as a donation to a nonprofit organization, charity, or school. Even bringing home a computer for your young children to hone their skills is better than adding to the ever-increasing scrap piles of old computers. While a two-year-old computer is a dinosaur to some people who need the latest models, the vast majority of computer users can make do with a computer from last year or even the year before that.

Along with independent recycling programs and businesses designed for that purpose, many manufacturers have instituted their own recycling programs. Dell, Apple, Acer, Gateway, HP, and Toshiba are just some of the manufacturers that now have such recycling programs. You may need to pay for shipping, but consider this part of your contribution to the environment. In addition, several states, have also instituted laws regarding e-waste disposal and many now have compliant programs available.

There is also a growing number of local computer recycling centers, which take in or buy computers for recycling, selling, or reusing parts. Look on a local web directory or even in the phone book for such centers near your business.

A couple of sources for recycling that you can visit online include Electronics Recycling Infrastructure Clearinghouse at **ecyclingresource.org** and Eco-Office, at **eco-office.com**. Look for companies that have locations near your office. Designate someone to be in charge of the recycling efforts, and make cartridge recycling and computer reuse part of your environmental plan for the future of your business.

WE CAN DO BETTER

While the United States is a major player when it comes to recycling computer hardware and printer cartridges, we can certainly do better, especially considering that we are the nation that uses the most computers in the world.

In 2007 alone, 248 million pounds of hardware and printer cartridges were recycled from Europe, the Middle East, and Africa; 170 million pounds were collected by Hewlett-Packard alone. The United States collected 65 million pounds of computer products in 2007 that were recycled, which is excellent, but we can do even better.

42 Quick Tip: Switch to E-Signatures

One of the roadblocks to the paperless office is documents that need to be signed, and there are numerous examples of such documents. We end up printing out tons of paper annually simply because we need to sign on the dotted line.

If you have ever signed on an electronic signature pad when paying by credit card (which typically resembles a small screen on which you write with a special soft-tip pen), you know what electronic signatures are. Using the right software, your signature can appear on any type of document and then be e-mailed accordingly. While some recipients will still insist on an actual signed piece of paper, a growing number of businesses are recognizing that electronic signatures are binding and can be accepted. In many cases, e-signatures can be used to fill complex application forms, saving plenty of paper and taking less time than the typical paperbound processing. The insurance industry is one example where this holds true.

In the meantime, e-signatures can make a difference to the environment. DocuSign, the leading web-based electronic signature company (**docusign.com**), notes on their website that 10 million pages saved equates roughly to:

- ♻ 2,500 trees
- ♻ 56,000 gallons of oil

DIRECT DEPOSIT

If you are not already doing so, join the thousands of companies that are paying employees by direct deposit. Using this very popular high-tech means of transferring paychecks into the savings or checking accounts of your staffers, you can save a bundle of paper on printing checks. Of course, you'll need to provide both options since some people will want a check in hand.

- ⚙ 450 cubic yards of landfill space
- ⚙ 595,000 kilowatts of energy
- ⚙ 1.04 million gallons of water

You'll also find a variety of signature pads that work with SigPlus software tools by checking out Topaz Systems at **topazsystems.com**.

While e-signatures alone won't make you much greener, if you can help encourage other companies to use this basic technology, the end result will be a big plus for the planet.

43 Recycle Cell Phones for the Planet and for Charity

A long with computers and cartridges, the newest wave of recyclable electronic products are cell phones. Since users are upgrading every year and a half, and some are looking for the latest in phones every year, there are now roughly 120 million cell phones being retired each year in the United States. Since less than 3 percent are ever actually reused by someone else, most end up in closets, drawers, or somewhere gathering dust. In time, however, people will accumulate more old cell phones than they have room for, and they too, will start going to landfills, unless the trend is averted before it becomes standard practice.

The concern is already growing very rapidly, as discarded cell phones account for nearly 65,000 tons of toxic waste each year. While there is no national legislation in place yet, some states have laws in place or legislation pending to make cell phone recycling mandatory. In California, retailers are required by law to accept retired cell phones at no charge for recycling purposes.

Along with the concern that landfills will be the destination for millions of cell phones, there is concern for the energy used to manufacture phones and the environment in which cell phones are produced. The process of mining for the coltan used in cell phones is detrimental to wildlife.

There are a few campaigns in place to discourage buyers from chasing the newest models as they roll off the production line. Just as you may not need the most recent bells and whistles available on a computer, you may also delay acquiring the newest cutting-edge cell phone. Of course, since companies do not control the personal cell phone buying habits of their employees, the best you can do is to encourage your staff to hold onto their current models longer and start a recycling program for cell phones.

You can launch a cell phone recycling program and make it a fundraiser for a worthwhile cause. Put someone in charge of the cell phone donation program, and together with this individual and your staff, you can determine which existing cell phone donation program you would like to be a part of. Or you can start your own program in conjunction with a charity in your neighborhood. Run the program for a certain amount of time—one month, 90 days, or a year—and then bring the phones to a cell phone recycling center where you will receive a check for the phones collected.

To bring in business, you can have this extend beyond employees to your customers as well, who can also bring in their obsolete cell phones. And don't forget to encourage employees to spread the word to people closest to them, as their own version of the friends and family plan.

Newer phones can collect upwards of $10, while most of the older models are worth $1, maybe $2. You may have some phones that are so obsolete they aren't worth any monetary amount, but may have recyclable parts. The earliest cell phones might be worthwhile to collectors who will someday sell them as antiques. Of course, it goes without saying that all of these phones should be inactive. The money earned will be presented to the organization of choice. Along with doing something positive and philanthropic, you can set an example for other businesses and reap some positive public relations as well. People like doing business with companies that are actively making a difference, and they typically feel positive about a company that is doing something good for the community.

For more about e-cycling cell phones, you can go to New Tech Recycling at **newtechrecycling.com** or US Recycle Ink at **usrecycleink.com**. For cell phones in particular, you might try Recellular at **recellular.com/recycling** or Eco-Cell at **eco-cell.org/ locate_recycler.asp**.

For charitable contributions, you can contact **RecycleForBreast-Cancer.org** or **phones4charity.org**. These are just a few of many websites you will find when searching for places to recycle your electronic equipment and donate it to charities.

44 Quick Tip: Use Rechargeable Batteries

A simple but effective means of keeping some of the 15 billion batteries discarded each year out of landfills is to buy rechargeable batteries for all of your battery-operated office devices. A rechargeable battery can be recharged and used several hundred times, which also provides cost-efficiency. In most digital cameras, rechargeable batteries will outperform their alkaline counterparts, and even though some cameras do drain batteries quickly, you will be able to simply recharge and use. While there is some energy expenditure with the recharging, it is significantly less of a factor than the enormous waste of non-rechargeable batteries. And, in recent years, with the proliferation of hand-held devices, Energy Star has begun rating battery chargers, so you can look for their label on the most energy-efficient models. Chargers can use significant energy in non-active modes and this is where the Energy Star models can be most effective, saving as much

FAST FACT

Nickel-metal hydride batteries (aka Ni-MH), as well as Lithium-ion (aka Li-ion) rechargeable batteries, are among the most highly-recommended, longest-lasting batteries you can buy today.

as 35 percent of the energy expenditure over other models. Of course, you can also go out and buy a solar battery charger and stay 100 percent green with your battery use. PowerFilm® makes portable solar-powered battery chargers that you can check out at Solar Direct (**solardirect.com**). You might also check out PDA Solar Battery Chargers from Silicon Solar Inc. (**siliconsolar.com**). You can also use an in-car charger which utilizes what would normally be wasted energy from the motor.

45 Quick Tip: Go With Voice Mail

While answering machines are most people's choice for home use, businesses, including very small ones, should opt for voice mail instead. A study by the German-based Wuppertal Institute determined that replacing 18 million conventional answering machines in Germany with voice mail would save around 788 GWh per year and 600,000 tons of greenhouse gas emissions. A report by The Daily Green (**thedailygreen.com**) estimated that if the United States switched from answering machines to voice mail, the energy savings would be equal to the savings of taking 250,000 cars off the roads.

Voice mail for business is also practical, as it allows a small business to enjoy a "big" business identity at a low monthly rate. Consumers are familiar with voice mail services, and often an answering machine implies a less professional service or company. In addition, there is greater versatility with voice mail, which you can tailor to your changing needs rather than buying a new answering machine for the latest features and adding more electronic equipment to the scrap piles. Also, consider that the shipping of answering machines can be minimized if there are fewer of them used for business.

While they are not a major drain of power, like many other modern electronic devices, answering machines do use electricity on a constant basis. Those that come with phones often use slightly less than standalone answering machines; however, they typically use energy as well, even when they are not in active operation.

Less Waste and a Cleaner Work Environment

46 Have a Waste Audit Done

You could use a tape measure for a personal "waist audit" to get an idea of how much weight you want to lose. For your business, however, a waste audit is a means of determining how much waste is produced by your company, how it is disposed of, and how much can be reused, recycled, or in some manner diverted from heading to a landfill.

You can do a waste audit on your own or look for the help of a consultant or someone who has spent significant time in waste management.

On your own, you can look at the amount you pay for waste disposal and how much weight is carted away. You can also count how many trash bins are filled and hauled off each week. Next, you will want to determine which items can be recycled or reused. Again, determine the weight of the recyclable items and then see how much total weight you can move from the disposal category to the recycling or reuse category. If your company is large enough, you can do this for each department, reviewing and analyzing how much waste can be moved from the discard to the recycle or reuse categories. In some cases, items that are recyclable are not being recycled. This can easily be rectified.

If the weight and subsequent bills for disposal are reduced, then you are on the right track. Often technological items are the first candidates for reuse, since giving something away to someone else who can utilize it certainly beats throwing it away.

Anne Bedarf of **GreenBlue.com** notes the importance of knowing what "away" means when referring to throwing something away. "A company called Sonoco Sustainability Solutions features waste reduction experts," explains Bedarf, referring to the $4 billion, 109-year-old business, which now features more than 300 locations and tremendous expertise in the area of reliable and innovative recycling solutions. Dedicated to diverting materials from landfills, Sonoco Sustainability Solutions (aka 3S) is one of a number of companies that can conduct a waste reduction audit in order to create a program specific to the needs of your company (**sonoco.com**).

Bedarf also recommends calling your local solid waste authority, management group, or a city or county sustainability coordinator, director, or environmental manager. You can also find consultants in waste management or pollution prevention who can help you get such an audit started. Consultants can provide advice on water and chemical usage as well as solid waste, and offer safer alternatives.

In the end, you will be able to downgrade the degree of waste that is not being either recycled or reused.

47 *Quick Tip: Reduce Holiday Party Waste*

Whether it's an end-of-the year holiday party or any other celebration throughout the year, it is still important to think green, and not only on St. Patrick's Day. Celebrations are wonderful times to bring your employees together and build teams, camaraderie, and a sense of unity. All of this is important for morale, production, dedication, and loyalty to the company, as well as providing some much needed time to blow off the steam that builds with the pressure of meeting deadlines, appeasing difficult customers, and working long hours.

Yet, even while—or especially while—celebrating, it's a good time to think green. Washable plates, cups, and utensils are better than plastic, but they also waste the water needed to wash them. One solution is to purchase biodegradable goods for your party, made of sugarcane, corn, or other vegetable starches that begin the biodegrading process within 24 hours.

You can also take a thrifty approach and see what you can utilize among the items already in your office for decorations. You'd be surprised at what you can come up with by using a little creativity. You can also start a party center in a corner of the break room where people put items they've come across during the year that might be usable at parties. Don't forget that plants can make better organic centerpieces that can go home with guests, rather than eco-unfriendly balloons or tinsel concoctions.

Also, remember to use recycled wrapping paper. If everyone simply opens gifts without totally destroying the paper, you can use the same wrapping paper several times over, make a joke out of it, and get into the habit of reusing the paper and bows again and again. If you really want to maintain a green theme, you can go with organic foods and beverages as well. You can find organic wine, made from 100 percent organically grown ingredients. Look at the labels and you'll find that organic domestic wines include the USDA organic seal (the certifying agency must be listed). This means no sulfites are added, though it can contain naturally occurring sulfites. Many such wines have received very good reviews from wine enthusiasts.

After the party comes the fun of cleaning up. Here, too, you can think ecologically by going with reusable cleaning materials over paper towels, and cleaning products that are organic-based rather than those filled with the toxic chemicals we've all come to know so well. Also, make sure you have clearly marked recycling bins, which should already be in your office.

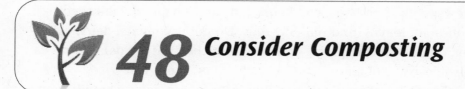

48 *Consider Composting*

You may ask, What is composting? Fair question. Answer: It is a process whereby biodegradable material, such as garden and kitchen waste, is converted, in the presence of readily available oxygen, into a stable material that can then be applied to land and soil to improve and enrich the nutrient content. It is a process of turning garbage into fertilizer for gardens, rather then sending it off to a landfill where it will benefit nothing and no one.

Compost consists largely of food scraps and yard waste, although a number of other types of garbage will fit into the category. As a fertilizer or soil nutrient, compost allows soil to hold more water. The result is that most plants, from flowers to vegetables, will grow better. Compost also provides food for microorganisms, which helps soil remain healthy and balanced.

It's not hard for businesses to utilize their garbage in a positive way. Compost bins are relatively inexpensive and composting is not a hard process to learn. You can purchase composting equipment, which includes a durable container with slots for air circulation, compartments for ingredients, and a cover. You can then put the compost bin on what is called an axle, which allows you to rotate it in order to mix your garbage. There is a strategy to composting that includes knowing what materials to mix into your garbage for best results. For example, you will want to use greens that disintegrate like vegetable peelings, melon rinds, apple cores, beans, and lettuce, along with what are referred to as browns, which are carbon-producing elements like wood chips, straw, bark, or dry leaves. Nitrogen, which provides the protein, and carbon, which provides energy for microbes, in the proper ratios will help turn your trash into compost. The best ratio is 25 parts brown matter to 1 part green matter, although it is not an exact science.

Other items that are good for composting include seaweed, newspapers, tea bags, coffee grounds or filters, corn stalks, corncobs, oak leaves, and pine needles. Do not use meats, dairy, cat litter, dog or cat droppings, or ashes from charcoal or coal. Weeds can also pose a problem.

For detailed information, you'll want to visit **compostguide.com** or check out "What is Composting?" at **wisegeek.com**. You may also want to look up composting on the EPA website, at **epa.gov/compost** where you can find environmental benefits, laws, and regulations regarding composting. Following a composting recipe, you'll be able to turn garbage into what is called humus (no, not the kind made from chick peas), and this is valuable source of nutrition can benefit your own green acreage or gardens, lawns, and fields in your community.

The U.S. Composting Council at **compostingcouncil.org**, can also prove helpful in your composting education. You might also purchase the book *Composting: A Practical Step by Step Guide* from Penguin Global Press or *Basic Composting: All the Skills and Tools You Need to Get Started* by Erich Ebeling.

Another option is to worm your way through the process by using vermicomposting, or worm composting. This process uses real earthworms, specifically red wigglers, or red earthworms, that will turn organic wastes into very high-quality compost. While an earthworm compost setup might not be practical outside a high-end chandelier store, it may work just fine outside a store selling outdoor camping and fishing gear.

Regardless of how you compost, you might consider this as a means of giving your garbage back to the earth and, in a sense, creating your own mini-recycling center.

49 *Share Your Waste*

Before you discard your old computers, office furniture, or anything else, you should look around at other businesses or community organizations that can utilize your items. This is a very basic type of recycling that does not involve recycling centers, but focuses on the reuse of products that can be beneficial and have a longer life span. In addition, you may find ways in which product waste can be utilized by other businesses. For example, many factories are now finding that the materials that are not used in the manufacturing process can be melted down and used for other purposes. By developing relationships with other businesses, you can lower their costs while lowering your carbon footprint by putting your unused items to work for another business. Even artists are potential sources for such materials, since many now make anything from jewelry to statues from discarded materials, particularly metals.

If your company has green acreage, you can even utilize natural materials for use by other businesses. An interesting example of sharing the waste comes from New Belgium Brewery, the organic beer makers in Fort Collins, Colorado. The brewery sits on a 25-acre campus of mostly agricultural land. As it turns out, the land has additional value for other small companies. Solex, a company that is working on utilizing algae for making biodiesel fuel, has found that they can utilize the nutrient-rich water on the grounds of the brewery, making this a supply stream (literally) for another business. Another company, Oberon, has installed a small treatment plant next to the brewery that will process wastewater and harvest sludge to create a high-protein fish food for aqua-farms. "We're finding that we can help smaller noncompetitive companies get set up," says Greg Owsley, Chief Branding Officer for the highly sustainable brewery.

Several years back, feathers from poultry plants became part of the production process for a company called Featherfiber, which used feather processing techniques mixed with natural and synthetic materials to make air filters, diapers, clothing, absorbent pads, wipes, insulation, and upholstery padding. Additionally, the quills left over, or the second generation of a waste product, were processed into proteins and then used to make shampoo and hair care items. The point is that at each level a use was found for what was otherwise seen as waste.

Part of your initiative to go greener should involve connecting with other businesses and determining how you can utilize resources

FAST FACT

You can also find your own uses for garbage. Nike teamed up with Phoenix Suns all-star guard Steve Nash to turn garbage into shoes. Nike's Trash Talk basketball shoe is made primarily from manufacturing waste materials that would normally be tossed into the garbage.

and research from one another to build more sustainable practices. Establishing a dialogue about sustainability with other businesses can serve as a means to build alliances, and working together for the good of the planet can have a greater impact than going it alone.

Also, remember, one company's garbage is another company's gold!

50 *Start an Anti-Litter Campaign*

Litter is a growing problem. Bags, bottles, and other forms of packaging that are so often discarded or left in parks or on beaches do not simply disappear. Too often they end up in forest areas where they affect wildlife, or in oceans and streams, where they often destroy the species that call these bodies of water home. It is estimated that nearly two million tons of plastic finds its way into the ocean every year.

While no single business can make a dent in the worldwide litter problem, your business can take the lead in preventing litter from causing damage in local lakes, streams, ponds, parks, and forests. Anti-litter campaigns can include your staff and community participants when you gather for cleanups and promote the anti-litter message.

You can also encourage people to use reusable bags and cups in your business. For example, if you own a coffee shop, restaurant, or bar, encourage your customers to bring in their own cups or mugs rather than use a new paper or Styrofoam cup each time they choose to take out a cup of coffee or a beer. Offer a free drink for the best-designed mug or cup each week, and you will encourage your customers to use reusable cups more often rather than paper or Styrofoam.

Taking on an anti-litter campaign and coupling it with a reuse and refill campaign is a win-win situation for the environment and

NORTH PACIFIC GYRE

To get an idea of the potential devastation accumulated litter can have, you need look no farther than the North Pacific Gyre, an area covering 10 million square miles in the Pacific Ocean comprised of clockwise swirling currents. Litter from beaches and ships—millions of tons of it—has accumulated in this gyre, which sits between California and Hawaii. The swirling mass is estimated to be significantly larger than the state of Texas. Needless to say, the result has affected and/or destroyed thousands of fish, along with numerous whales, sea lions, sea birds, and more than 200 other species that inhabit the ocean.

for your business, which will be seen as spearheading a very important and often overlooked environmental activity. Yes, there are numerous ways in which we can help the planet by employing new recycling techniques, newly created building materials, and energy-efficient technology. There are also basic efforts that can make a very significant difference in a community, such as getting the message out that littering is not acceptable.

51 *Clean Green*

The environment notwithstanding, your health, and that of everyone in your office, store, or factory should provide the impetus to use greener cleaning products. A greener business also means a healthier environment for everyone involved in your company, including your customers.

For years, businesses have used cleaning products composed of dangerous chemicals, which kill germs and shine surfaces while releasing toxins into the air before being discarded into landfills as hazardous waste. While such products are still on the market, a rapidly increasing number of concerned business owners and managers have opted to clean up their office environments by switching to non-toxic, less dangerous alternatives.

Along with ammonia, borax, and good old baking soda, there are green cleaning products that can do the same job as the high-powered, high-toxic cleaners, and many are certified by Green Seal, which evaluates cleaning (and other) products and gives their seal of approval to those that meet their high standards (**greenseal.org**). In developing environmental standards and certifying products, Green Seal follows the Guiding Principles and Procedures for Type I Environmental Labeling adopted by the International Organization for Standardization (ISO 14024).

For your purposes, you will be seeking cleaning products that:

- Have no volatile organic compounds (VOCs)
- Have no ingredients derived from petroleum
- Have no chlorine bleach
- Have a neutral pH
- Have no phosphates
- Have no artificial fragrances or dyes
- Are nontoxic to humans, animals, and plants
- Are biodegradable
- Come in containers that are recyclable, refillable, or reusable
- Are made from naturally derived ingredients from sustainable sources

You can also use microfiber mops and cloths for cleaning. In addition to seeking out environmentally safe cleaning products and supplies, you also need to be proactive in regard to maintaining cleaning product safety. For example, containers should be closed tightly and stored in one location, and any spills or leaks should be cleaned up immediately. If you implement a simple plan by which cleaning crew members, or in small offices, your employees themselves, know exactly what is expected when they are cleaning anywhere within the business, you can avoid future contamination. You should be sure to state in your cleaning plan that any potential pollutant should not be poured down the drain and into the sewer system. And finally, even with greener cleaning products, remind anyone using them to take any safety precautions that are recommended, such as wearing gloves, keeping a window open for ventilation, and always washing their hands after using a cleaning product.

Greener cleaning is a very simple, yet frequently overlooked way to benefit the environment, the indoor air quality of your facility, and ultimately the health and well-being of your staff and yourself.

52 *Maintain a High Level of Indoor Air Quality*

Indoor pollution is becoming an area of greater concern. On a regular basis, your work environment is infiltrated by the residue from:

- ♻ Cleaning products
- ♻ Packing materials
- ♻ Technology
- ♻ Foods and chemicals used on agricultural products
- ♻ Dust and particles from manufacturing products

Add to this anything brought in on the clothing of your staff, and you get the idea—a lot of potential pollutants fill the air in most work establishments.

You can improve the indoor air quality of your place of business. One option is to place air filters in air return vents and other locations. You may already have filters in your HVAC system. Filters are designed to catch the particles that would otherwise pass through. You need to clean or replace filters regularly. HEPA (High Energy Particulate Air) filters and ULPA (Ultra Low Penetration Air) filters are DEA-approved and can capture dust and other airborne particles. If you are in manufacturing, you may very likely need air filtering systems that meet government clean air regulations.

Then there are the actual purifiers. Ionizing and ozone air purifiers are most commonly hyped. The concept of ionizing is to use what is called a corona discharge to create an electronic field and ultimately draw particles out of the air and/or neutralize them. Ozone generators work in a similar manner. The problem, however, is that they release ozone into the atmosphere, which can be irritating to humans, and has been billed "indoor smog" by some critics. While filters such as HEPA are EPA-approved, ozone generators are not. In fact, you will find a number of articles questioning whether ozone generators are purifying air at all, or creating more dangerous air.

One type of air filtering method that has been gaining greater attention is the UV air purifier, which uses ultraviolet light to destroy airborne bacteria and air contaminants by damaging the DNA of microorganisms and rendering them harmless. Once again, there is the potential for levels of ozone to be produced by such lamps. Bottom line: be leery and cautious of indoor air purification systems. Go with EPA-approved filters instead.

An important step in maintaining indoor air quality is to make it part of your office or business culture. Therefore, while you can incorporate air filters in your facility, you'll also want to establish some good, old-fashioned means of maintaining cleaner air. For example:

- Make sure vents are not blocked
- Have HVAC systems cleaned periodically
- Maintain a no-smoking policy, with smokers relegated to outdoor areas only
- Clean up all spills (of any type) quickly
- Make sure water leaks are reported and repaired quickly, since standing water can promote the growth of mold and fungi
- Make sure food is stored in airtight containers
- Make sure garbage is properly disposed of and people do not keep food in their desks or work areas where it can create odors or unsanitary conditions
- Use only environmentally friendly (green) cleaning supplies

Improved indoor air quality can have a very positive affect on employee productivity.

53 *Stop Junk Mail From Coming to Your Office*

Junk mail is an incredible waste of paper, and energy. It is estimated that more than 60 billion dollars is spent on junk mail annually, with an energy output equal to that of three million cars. You can make an effort to stop it.

Another way of cleaning up your office is to rid yourself of some of this junk. The first step is to talk with your vendors, distributors, and all organizations and associations to which you belong, and let them know you do not want them to give your business contact information to any of the random mailing list distribution and rental companies. You can also contact the Direct Marketing Association and register with their Mail Preference Service. Another option is to join the DMA's do-not-mail list at **dmachoice.org/MPS/proto1.php**. It can become tricky, because you want your business to be marketed and your name to be out there for the public to see. However, you do not want to be solicited by anyone and everyone selling all sorts of things through the mail.

By setting up standard procedures for reaching and doing business with your company, and letting it be known that you will not do business with junk-mail solicitors, you can begin to halt the tide of junk mail—slowly, but surely. Another place for help with unwanted mail, especially if you are receiving mail for former employees, is the Ecological Mail Coalition, at **ecologicalmail.org** or **1-800-620-3975**.

Homebased business owners are often besieged by junk mail, since the thinking is that such business owners are looking to grow and expand. It is extremely important to monitor to whom you provide your mailing information. If you call the 1-800 number provided on junk mail or find the company website, you can politely ask to be taken off of all mailing lists. There are also some organizations that will stop your junk mail for a small fee, such as Stop the Junk Mail, at **stopthejunkmail.com** where you can get help for just $20 a year.

Section 8. Less Waste and a Cleaner Work Environment

In some cases, you may at least be able to move junk snail mail to electronic communications, which is still a problem, but wastes far less energy and doesn't destroy trees.

The key is to be proactive. Have a policy that you will not do business with junk mailers (or spammers) and make it a point of letting them know by phone or e-mail. In the meantime, reuse junk mail as scrap paper and for packing boxes, rather than using Styrofoam peanuts, so at least it is not a complete waste.

The more businesses that stand up to junk mailers and spammers, the less likely it is that they will continue to be as great a burden as they are today.

SECTION 9

Shipping and Products

54 Work With Green Vendors and Suppliers

I f Wal-Mart can do it, so can you. The widely publicized Wal-Mart scorecard was designed to make sure that the major retail chain was working with what they considered to be the greenest vendors, based on their own set of criteria. Other businesses, including yours, can make the same efforts in an attempt to use environmentally safer products, pass on sustainable merchandise to your customers, and have an overall greener business environment, while, in most cases, saving money.

The practice of working with environmentally sensitive vendors and suppliers is relatively new and thus far there are no strict definitions for what makes a business fit the bill. In fact, the scope of environmental concerns is so broad that any number of factors may or may not be used in such criteria.

Therefore, it is up to you to set some standards and, in essence, determine what a passing grade is for your choice of vendors and suppliers. Of course, these vendors and suppliers will need to fall in line with the needs of your business as well as your budget.

Here are some criteria to consider:

- ♻ Does the vendor-supplier have a recycling and/or reuse policy in place?
- ♻ Does the vendor-supplier have an energy reduction policy in place?
- ♻ Are the vendor-supplier's products made from recyclable materials?
- ♻ Does the vendor-supplier practice energy conservation at their business site? (You can make a separate list of what you consider energy conservation, ranging from wind-turbine power to Energy Star office and business equipment.)

Section 9. Shipping and Products

- Are toxic or environmentally unfriendly chemicals used in the manufacture of the product or the product itself?
- Does the vendor-supplier use environmentally friendly, sustainable shipping materials? Do they use excessive shipping materials?
- Does the vendor-supplier utilize parts and products shipped from long distances (that could be found locally)?
- Is the vendor-supplier within 500 miles of your business? 100 miles? (This will depend on the availability or scarcity of the products in question.)
- Does the vendor-supplier donate money and/or time to sustainable initiatives and organizations? Do they have any involvement in social or environmental groups or activities?
- Does the vendor-supplier pay employees a living wage and do they have any benefits? Remember, environmental concerns go hand in hand with social responsibility.

These are just some of the criteria you can look at and evaluate when deciding between various vendors or suppliers. Keep in mind that you will come across some greenwashers—companies that make unsubstantiated or misleading claims about the environmental benefits of their products, services, technology, or company policies. While you may not want to give a vendor or supplier the third degree, you will want to ask at least some of these questions to determine the type of response you receive. You can and should also do some research into any companies with which you intend to do business.

Vendors and suppliers utilizing sustainable business practices are usually more than happy to share with you what steps they have taken to conserve energy and create (and ship) environmentally friendly products. Most business owners who are invested in ecological concerns are proud of their accomplishments, while those who are not buying into the green movement are usually more obvious, skirting questions or providing little information. It's all about building relationships with people who "get it," and they are becoming easier and easier to find. When you do find such companies, let them know you appreciate their efforts. Many businesses have teamed up on initiatives and have marketed products and concepts based on their joint belief in sustainable practices. Vendors and suppliers at the top of the Wal-Mart lists are not only working with Wal-Mart, but generating attention from other companies. Therefore, an environmentally positive reputation can emerge from such relationships. And, it's not just large companies that can monitor with whom they choose to work. Smaller businesses like Nau, the Oregon-based clothing manufacturer, carefully monitor, with help from an outside auditor, the companies with whom they align themselves.

Needless to say, quality and price of merchandise are always a concern when working with a vendor or supplier, even a green one. If a business, sustainable or not, is producing substandard materials or charging too much for their products, you will still look elsewhere—that's business.

Note: Along with searching the web for your specific product needs, you can check with environmental groups and any local environmental government agencies, where you may get information about, and recommendations for, such companies. Trade unions and even your local chamber of commerce may also point you in the right direction.

55 *Quick Tip: Avoid Shipping Air*

In the cruise industry, different seasons mean different cruise offerings in various parts of the world. Therefore, boats that are handling Caribbean cruises may be rerouted to European destinations for several months and then brought back for Caribbean cruises during another season. Rather than having empty ships making the journey while switching routes, the industry created what are called repositioning cruises, where people actually pay for and enjoy a

Section 9. Shipping and Products

cruise that is not a designated route, but is actually the repositioning of the ship to another part of the world. While there is some debate as to how green cruises are, the concept of not sailing empty ships spills over to businesses and their shipping needs.

Most often, after you receive products and packages, the truck or van then returns to the warehouse, distribution center, or factory with no contents; they are "shipping air."

While it is not easy to control the actions of other businesses, you might consider if your own business can make the adjustments necessary to avoid shipping air. Naturally, you can't ship what does not need to be shipped. However, you could creatively team up with other businesses to take their goods back to the general area where your truck or van is headed.

If, for example, your New York City stores are getting merchandise shipped from your Menlo Park, New Jersey warehouse, you could:

- Have all the returns ready to go back to Menlo Park from your stores at the same time.
- Look for other businesses that have items to ship to nearby areas in New Jersey and can utilize your services for a nominal fee; they would save money on transport and the truck or van would not return empty.

The more that two-way shipping replaces one-way distribution, the fewer vehicles need to be utilized. Clearly, this is a plus for the environment by limiting the emissions from x number of wasted trips.

Even home business owners can utilize the same philosophy. For example, if you work from home and need to drop off business materials at a client's office, why not at least combine the excursion with picking up your dry cleaning or some other errand, which could be business or personal?

Take a page from the cruise lines and make your transport work both ways. You'll also appreciate the savings on gas, and so will the environment.

56 *Work With Local Suppliers*

Long-distance shipping is a significant form of energy waste and typically increases the cost of doing business and selling products. Money spent on gas used to transport items long distances results in higher shipping costs, especially as fuel prices continue to rise. Temperature-sensitive items, such as foods that need to be shipped in refrigerated trucks, can be even costlier to ship over longer distances.

The solution is to change your buying habits in favor of local suppliers whenever possible. Many restaurants in farm regions of the country are already making a greater effort to patronize local growers, while some companies are utilizing the craftsmanship of local builders and carpenters, rather than ordering furniture online from distant locations.

Some businesses, such as car dealerships, won't find auto manufacturers in their backyard. However, even car dealerships need to furnish their showrooms and offices. Thanks to the worldwide availability of products and resources through the internet, the globe has shrunk and it has become easier to have anything shipped anywhere. We need to limit our indulgence in this sweeping availability to the purchase of unique items that cannot be found locally. Remember, you can also use the internet and other resources to find local vendors and suppliers.

Look carefully at what you use in your business and what you sell, including:

- Supplies
- Equipment and technology
- Parts used for manufacturing
- Products sold

Which of these need to be imported from a great distance, and which can be purchased locally? Many business owners use a supplier out of habit, and don't consider that materials are being shipped 500 miles or that the same materials can be found within a 100-mile radius.

Developing relationships with local suppliers can not only curtail unnecessary shipping, but can sometimes allow you to cross-promote your business with theirs and serve as a PR boost for both companies. You will also expedite the process of receiving goods, and in the case of errors or technical problems, have a supplier nearby to deal with rather than someone hundreds or thousands of miles away, which is as time-consuming as it is wasteful. You are also supporting your local community or your state by patronizing local suppliers.

Of course, all this being said, you need to know that the quality of the products and the business practices of the local companies with which you do business meet your standards, and that the prices are fair. A company down the block could have exactly what you need, except that the workmanship is shoddy or the company is polluting the environment. In short, local isn't always preferable, but it is certainly worth exploring.

57 Make Your Internal Shipping Needs Greener

It's one thing to look for local vendors and suppliers, and another to consolidate and/or condense your own shipping needs.

When minimizing your own shipping needs, you have far greater control over the matter than when you work with outside vendors and suppliers. You are essentially coordinating all aspects of the journey between your factory and your distribution centers or perhaps your warehouse and retail outlets.

Clif Bar & Company lowered their own carbon footprint of shipping from bakeries to distribution centers from 508 tons of CO_2 in

2003 to 15 tons in 2007. They did this by setting up new distribution centers and locations that were more convenient to the stores where they sell their products and by switching to sustainable biodiesel fuel in their trucks. If it is not possible to move your distribution center or warehouse, it may be possible to condense shipping so that you use fewer trucks, but each truck carries a full load and travels at low-congestion times.

Other businesses are also considering where they can better situate their distribution centers for quicker and greener internal shipping. Some smaller companies have teamed up to hire independent truckers to carry products for a few businesses at once. This works if you have other small businesses nearby who are all shipping to similar areas.

Naturally, you will not want to inconvenience your valuable customer who needs a part for installation that just happens to be somewhere in your warehouse. However, many businesses today are rethinking the need to have their drivers scurrying around when there are alternatives. Some companies with small items to whisk back and forth have opted for more bike messengers and fewer small trucks and vans on the road.

Of course, some businesses find that shipping directly from the factory to the customer eliminates the need to ship to middle destinations, whether it is a warehouse or distribution center. Depending on the nature of your business, this might be another consideration.

In the end, less internal shipping can make a huge difference to the environment and save you money at those high-cost gas pumps.

58 *Minimize Excess Inventory*

Many retail stores suffer from excess inventory, which can not only put a dent in the bottom line, but can also be environmentally insensitive. The excess shipping, packaging, and costs used to

Section 9. Shipping and Products

store such inventory are all energy wasters. In addition, depending on your type of business, you need to figure out what to do with excess inventory so it does not require extra energy to maintain it.

Today, there are many options to sell off excess inventory, including of course, eBay. The easier solution is to avoid becoming overstocked in the first place. By controlling and managing inventory effectively, you can avoid being in such situations.

Of course, this is no easy task, and many companies take time through trial and error before determining exactly how much they expect to sell in how much time. However, it is important in maintaining inventory control that you set the tone with the proper attitude. As with a strong customer service policy, everyone needs to be committed to following the inventory system you decide to implement, whether it includes the latest in inventory software or a manual system that has worked for generations. Keep in mind, the best inventory management system is one which everyone can understand in order to minimize errors and keep accurate counts of merchandise ordered and sold. Employee training is a significant aspect of inventory management and control in retail, since your employees will be the ones selling, stocking, and restocking your merchandise.

Take time and answer questions as you train your employees. A simple handout or e-mail list cannot replace in-person training. Cycle counting, which refers to ongoing counting of your inventory, should be used to keep you abreast of your numbers, and software should be used as a tool for measuring and alerting you to the need to reorder.

From counting and measuring to the latest state-of-the-art inventory software to systems and formulas, you can make inventory control much easier today than ever before. You should look into inventory management systems and make sure you utilize one to make your life easier.

However, there's one final element in controlling inventory and avoiding overruns.

Have you ever walked into a privately owned shop and talked with a longtime owner? Someone who's been running the place for a year? Once you get him or her started, the owner can tell you all sorts of great stories about their busy seasons, quiet seasons, and the last-second sale they made before shutting their doors for Christmas Eve. Owners know what sells, when it will sell, and why it sells. They can tell you what they no longer order and why they don't. In short, they know their inventory like the backs of their hands.

This knowledge and experience comes with understanding what you are selling, who your customers are, what they want and when they want it, as well as what they don't want and why. This is gained from inventory analysis, which comes from keeping a keen eye on all that is going on in your business.

Reviewing your previous inventory numbers and learning to order and reorder accordingly can be a major energy saver. Ultimately, you will be better managing the supply chain by not sitting on wasted inventory. In addition, by taking a portion of your business online, you can order as the need arises.

Infor's EAM (Enterprise Asset Management) is one of many software programs designed to assist in the flow of information through the supply chain and can be of assistance.

For more information, go to **infor.com/solutions/eam**, You might also look at Idalica's Retail Management System with POS at **idalica.com**, or Retail Pro by One Step Retail Solutions at **onestepretail.com**.

59 *Revamp Your Products—Get Greener*

I f you are in the manufacturing end of business, this is a must for staying competitive in an ever-evolving marketplace. Green is the color of choice today, and if you are not making an effort to make your products environmentally friendly, you may be left behind.

In some industries, government regulations are forcing the hand of engineers, scientists, and manufacturers to go greener. The auto industry, for example, has to conform to regulations regarding emissions. In many industries, however, meeting minimal government guidelines only means scratching the surface. It is therefore up to ownership and management to launch top-down initiatives that motivate the research and development teams to make environmentally friendlier products a top priority.

As cited elsewhere in the book, many computer companies are looking for ways to minimize the energy output and maximize the efficiency of their products. (Find information on buying green computers in Subsection 40.)

What are greener products?

"The question you want to ask yourself is: How close are my products to nature?" notes environmental journalist Trish Riley, author of the *Complete Idiot's Guide to Green Living*.

As Riley points out, you want to determine how sustainable your products are. In other words, if they are made with synthetic chemicals, you are not there yet.

While new products can be developed with environmentally friendly materials already in place, the need to revamp and recreate new greener versions of existing products is a greater challenge. You do not want to lose the familiarity customers have with your products.

Therefore, research and development needs to carefully rework products and packaging with new components and materials, to see if they can recreate familiar products with natural materials. In some cases, it works while in other situations, it is very hard to do.

Nonetheless, through trial and error, we are seeing more mainstream manufacturers take the initiative to go greener with their products. Even Clorox, whose cleaning products have stood the test of time for 20 years, instituted Green Works, a new line of cleaning products that are made from coconuts and lemon oil. The new cleaners are designed to be biodegradable and nonallergenic, and are packaged in recyclable bottles. Plus, they are not tested on animals. If a cleaning product manufacturer can make the effort to go green, it behooves other businesses to do the same. When familiar products cannot be made with organic materials, you might opt to create an alternative line, as many companies have done, and offer one line of products that is familiar and another that is greener.

While some large corporations tend to shy away from tinkering with success, the market is shifting, and in time, many such companies will be forced by consumer demand to compete on a greener playing field. Beer makers at Anheuser-Busch and Miller introduced organic products in response to a growing interest in organic beer, which was spurred on, in part, by microbreweries.

Even in the fashion world, you'll find a new line of organic denim jeans for women from eco-designer Tierra Del Forte, who also launched Project Rejeaneration, allowing customers to return their used Del Forte jeans for inspired reuse. You can always follow the example of Teko Socks, a Colorado-based company, and only utilize materials that will make your products sustainable. Teko makes socks from organic cotton, wool from a family farm in Tasmania, and/or recycled polyester made from old soda bottles and industrial waste.

If you're making towels, how about using bamboo? Yes, bamboo. An innovative company, Pure Fiber, took the idea and made naturally hypoallergenic, anti-microbial, and odor-resistant towels that many customers compare to silk or cashmere for softness.

The point is, you can make almost anything with organic and reusable ingredients if you have the impetus to do so. Since most businesses spend a great amount of time searching for that competitive edge, taking the initiative to green your products may be a good way to move to the forefront of your specialty. In an age where your products can go head to head with those of larger corporations on the internet, you can achieve an advantage if you can promote yourself for being greener.

60 Think Bio-Plastics

Whether you are buying, selling, or manufacturing materials made from plastic, you can make the switch from petroleum-based plastics, which are non-biodegradable, to more earth-friendly plastics. New plastics from organic, renewable sources can not only be environmentally beneficial, but will save you money in the long run, thanks to the high price of petroleum. Considering that over 80 million tons of oil is used to make plastic annually in the U.S. alone, you can see where more environmentally friendly grades of plastic can be a significant benefit from a cost standpoint.

There are numerous sources for bio-plastics. In recent years, the Cornell University Research Group discovered they could make plastics using citrus fruits, such as oranges, along with carbon dioxide. Meanwhile, a study from the Royal Institute of Technology in Sweden illustrated how plastic could be made from shrimp shells and assorted types of garbage. Cornstarch, pea-starch, and vegetable oil have become the more traditional means of plastic making in this nontraditional setting. The field continues to grow and major players, such as Dupont and ADM, are continuing to explore and develop new and better bio-plastics. The new bio-plastics are used, in some cases, along with more traditional petroleum-based plastic for added strength and durability. In other instances, bio-plastics are used on their own.

Among the many companies producing and utilizing the new bio-plastics is Toyota. They are using these plastics in various parts on their cars. Wal-Mart is using bio-plastics in their packaging. Food packaging companies are also finding uses for these newer, earth-friendly plastics.

Some methods used to create and market bio-plastics are not fully green, and there are still concerns about the biodegradability of this evolving product. Bio-plastics are a step in the right direction for the earth-conscious entrepreneur and his or her customers. While the research continues to develop, you can look into alternatives to traditional plastic in the products you buy, sell, and manufacture. You can find more on bio-plastics at *Bioplastics* magazine (**bioplasticsmagazine.com**).

Transportation, Travel, and Telecommuting

61 Make the Switch to Flex Fuel or Hybrid Cars, Vans, and Trucks

I f you use vehicles for your business, not to mention for personal use, it's time to consider investing in low-emission, hybrid, or flex fuel cars, vans, and trucks. The United States consumes 20.1 million barrels of oil every day; 70 percent of that is for transportation. If you've seen the price of gas lately, you can understand why making the switch to an environmentally friendly means of fuel, not only makes sense for the planet, but also for the wallet.

Flexible-fuel vehicles (FFV) typically use a mixture of fuel in one tank or have separate tanks for individual types of fuel. This allows the driver to switch back and forth between traditional oil-based gas and alternative ethanol-based gas, which is often made from 85 percent ethanol and 15 percent gasoline (known as E85). General Motors, Chrysler, and Ford Motor Company have all produced millions of vehicles capable of running on E85. The problem is that this type of fuel is not easy to find. In fact, it's darn near impossible. The government's ongoing dependence on foreign oil and the need to maintain close political ties with large oil companies has not made it any easier for the average person to make the switch to environmentally friendlier fuel. In fact, according to the National Ethanol Vehicle Coalition, of the 170,000 service stations in the United States, less than 1 percent sell E85.

In California, as of 2007, where there are over 250,000 flex fuel vehicles on the road, there are only two—that's right, two!—public service stations selling E85. In New Jersey, as of 2007, not one gas station sold E85. Therefore, even if you own a flex fuel vehicle, you are almost forced to use gasoline because there are no government incentives for stations to carry E85.

Section 10. Transportation, Travel, and Telecommuting

The other most common way to improve gas mileage while decreasing gas emissions is to go with a hybrid vehicle. The term *hybrid*, which has become very popular these days, means a mix of two components. We've seen hybrids in investing, where mutual funds take on different investment components, and hybrid golf clubs that mix the features of irons and woods.

Hybrid cars, vans, and trucks combine internal combustion engines with electric motors powered by batteries. The combination allows the electric motor and batteries to help the conventional engine operate more efficiently, cutting down on fuel use. Conversely, the combustion engine boosts what would be the limited driving range of a solely electric-powered vehicle. As a result, you can get 20 to 30 more miles per gallon than the standard car that runs only on gasoline. Most hybrids also have engine shut-off capacity, which means the engine shuts off when the car is idling, thus saving gas and limiting excessive emissions when you're waiting at traffic lights, caught in stop-and-go traffic, or stuck in any kind of vehicular queue.

With most vehicles, there are a variety of possibilities; this is true of hybrids as well. Therefore, you will want to do your homework when you are shopping for a hybrid car, van, or truck.

In the not too distant future, vehicles with advanced "clean" diesel engines will also be available. The noisy, smelly diesel engines of the past are refined and ready for wider use. Dodge, Ford, and Toyota all announced plans to offer new clean diesel engines in their light-duty (half-ton) pickups in 2009, or shortly thereafter. Diesel fuel also provides superior fuel economy. If you are using light-duty trucks in your business, it's worth keeping an eye on the advancements made in diesel engine innovations and forthcoming models.

It's not just for trucks. In 2009, Mercedes will be offering a chiseled 2009 GLK featuring a small, but powerful, diesel engine. The 2.2-liter, four-cylinder is a fully modern, clean diesel that meets tough new U.S. emissions standards. BMW will also put diesel power into their X5 SUV and their most popular car, the 3-Series, while other leading auto manufacturers will follow suit.

Section 10. Transportation, Travel, and Telecommuting

Despite the enhanced power of the modern engine, progress in creating fuel-efficient cars has moved along slowly, in part because the big oil companies like "taking you for a ride." However, pressure from advocacy groups and those politicians who "get it" is triggering ongoing changes in the automobile industry.

For your part, whether you have one company car or a fleet of pickup trucks and/or vans, you can explore flex fuel and hybrid options as they become more available from leading manufacturers. There are several hybrid models that have come to the forefront in 2008, with their 2009 models soon to follow.

Included are:

- **The 2008 Ford Escape Hybrid**. In the $25k to $28k price range, the Escape gets from 28 to 32 MPG and incorporates a 2.3-liter, 4-cylinder engine, with front and four-wheel drive options available. The Escape is a true hybrid and can propel itself for short distances at low speeds running only on its electric motor. The Ford Mercury Mariner compact SUV is almost identical in terms of engine design.
- **The 2008 Lexus RX 400h**. A more elegant entry, in the $41k to $43k price range, the Lexus SUV has an EPA MPG of 27-33, a 3.3-liter V6 engine and a continuously variable transmission. Additionally, the rear wheels are driven entirely by the hybrid's electric motors; there is no mechanical connection to the transmission.
- **The 2008 Honda Civic GX NGV**. With a base price of under $25k and a tax credit of $4,000, this model is a very popular option, reaching over 40 mph on the highway.
- **2008 Toyota Prius**. The most popular and beloved hybrid, now in its tenth year, the Prius offers superb fuel economy and lists for under $22k. The 2008 EPA combined city/highway rating is 46 mpg, making this a very good choice.

These are just four of the many hybrid vehicles currently available, or on the horizon, from General Motors, Ford, Honda, Nissan, and Toyota.

62 Think Green Tires

Whether you drive your car to and from your own small business or you own a fleet of cars and trucks, tire care can benefit the environment.

First, one of the simplest steps in tire maintenance is keeping your tires inflated at the proper pressure. How could this possibly help the environment? Well, for starters, each vehicle that drives 10,000 miles annually on under-inflated tires is using an extra 120 gallons of gas every year. At gas prices of $4 and up per gallon, that's an additional expense of nearly $500 per vehicle. Now, consider a fleet of 10 cars, vans, or trucks for your business and you are using an additional 1,200 extra gallons of gas a year and spending nearly $5,000 more, simply by not keeping the tires on your vehicles properly inflated. According to **fueleconomy.org**, "You can also improve your gas mileage by around 3.3 percent by keeping your tires inflated to the proper pressure."

Also, under-inflated tires are a likely cause of many SUV rollover accidents.

Along with checking air pressure, you also need to monitor the weight of your vehicles to be sure that you do not overload trucks and vans carrying your products.

The other side of the green tire equation is what happens to tires when they are put out to pasture. The problem is, too many tires are simply left lying around or dumped. In fact, it is estimated that nearly 300 million tires are dumped every year. Many end up in landfills and many are burned, emitting significant amounts of toxic air pollution into the environment, not to mention large amounts of polycyclic aromatic hydrocarbons. Even recycling centers, while well-intentioned, are not always handling tires properly. You need to see what will be done with the tires you leave at a recycling center.

Tires can be recycled into floor mats, planters, safety materials for playgrounds, washers for faucets, soles for shoes and sneakers, safety floor covering, tire swings, and various other products. There are plenty of creative uses for old tires; in fact, people have even filled in the middle, added legs and created some funky-looking tables, while others have used tires as planters. Again, find out what the options are and recycle old tires accordingly. If you find a recycling center that you like, spread the word and consider collecting used tires for recycling purposes. Remember, you can recycle for your community and enhance your business profile at the same time.

Additionally, you can now buy reconstructed and remolded tires. Check out Green Diamond Tires Company at **greendiamondtire. com**. They are a small, environmentally conscious tire company that uses new technology to make tires that last longer than many of their counterparts. After all, the longer your tires last, the fewer discarded tires there will be to pile up each year.

63 *Get Environmental Roadside Assistance and Use Green Travel Services*

Becoming a green company also takes shape in the associations that you support with your membership. For example, you can sign yourself and your employees up for green roadside assistance as a greener alternative to AAA. Better World Club (**Betterworldclub.com**) supports alternative modes of transportation and is dedicated to balancing economic goals with social and environmental responsibility. One percent of the company's annual revenues are directed toward environmental clean-up activities.

Better World provides full roadside assistance for vehicles, including bicycles, plus discounts for hybrid or biodiesel car rentals. The club also offers TravelCool partner program which promotes eco-friendly travel options to all members and provides information on sustainable travel practices.

When travel planning, you'll also want to know that there are eco-conscious travel agents and businesses available to help you. By moving your business travel to environmentally conscious booking agents, you are putting your travel dollars to better use environmentally. Santa Barbara-based **GreenTravelPartners.com** is an example of such a travel program designed to put money toward environmental preservation projects, in addition to saving businesses money on airfare, hotels, and car rentals. They also add profit-sharing opportunities for your company.

The more you align yourself with eco-friendly businesses and encourage their support of environmental concerns, the more immersed your business will become in the green culture. Additionally, your business travelers can learn what constitutes eco-friendly business travel. Be careful, however, to research the travel agency or club before signing on. As is the case in all industries, there are greenwashers who claim to be supporting environmental change, but are not actively doing so.

While The International Ecotourism Society (TIES) primarily supports tourism and leisure travel, you can also utilize their services for your small business needs, or simply to learn more about what eco-travel is all about. Their website at **ecotourism.org** provides a comprehensive look at sustainable travel that applies to travelers across the board.

You may also want to find green hotels by going to **environmentallyfriendlyhotels.com**. Finally, keep in mind that while auto travel (even with hybrids) burns fuel, cars are more environmentally friendly than air travel. So, you might opt to drive for short-destination business trips and take passengers when several employees share the same destination.

64 Encourage Alternative Forms of Commuting

If you consider the emissions from some 30 billion gallons of gas wasted each year by commuters sitting in traffic, you can understand the need for alternatives to the age-old concept of each employee driving alone to work every day. Outside a handful of major cities, driving is the primary means of commuting for nearly 90 percent of American workers. This has been the case since the mid-twentieth century when major highways began connecting towns and cities. As it became easier for people to commute to and from their places of work, the suburbs emerged and commuting became a way of life.

The problem today is that there are simply too many cars on the roads and too few people willing to make the necessary changes to limit the excess exhaust emissions that result from such an over-reliance on the automobile.

Although it is encouraged by many local municipalities with carpool lanes, carpooling remains one underutilized form of saving energy. Vanpooling with a designated (hired) driver is another alternative that is growing slightly in popularity. Large companies may subsidize the entire cost, while small businesses may have riders pay a minimal fee that amounts to less than paying for gas to commute to and from work on a daily basis.

One step that a growing number of businesses are taking is rewarding employees who use alternate forms of transportation. For example, Advanced Micro Devices (AMD) in Austin, Texas issues bus passes to all employees who use mass transit and rewards employees who carpool or vanpool with gift cards to local businesses.

Safeco Insurance offers subsidies and incentives to employees who use any of the 80 active vanpools they have set up throughout the country. New Belgium Brewery encourages biking to and from work by giving each employee who has been with the company for a year a bicycle. Nice.

Many small businesses are helping their employees set up carpools and vanpools and even encouraging bike riding with incentives such as free lunches, flex schedules, once-a-week telecommuting options, gift cards, and other perks.

While it's not practical for all companies, some businesses provide an incentive to walk or bike to work by setting up showers, lockers, and private changing areas. To encourage biking and walking, businesses have also helped set up buddy systems, where they help arrange for two or more people living in the same area to travel together.

If you'd like an easy-to-manage means of arranging your carpooling that rewards those who embrace alternative transportation, you might contact RideSpring (**ridespring.com**). Since the toughest part of starting and maintaining a carpool program is actually organizing it, RideSpring takes the onus off the business by providing software to handle the task. They also have a means of tracking the energy savings of your alternative commuters.

You can also look into Zipcar or Flexcar (**zipcar.com**, **flexcar.com**) as a means of having cars on hand for employees who need them. Both of these are innovative ways of having a car available when necessary, and yes, they are low-emission, fuel-efficient vehicles. Unlike a rental car, which is more costly and needs to be picked up at a specific location, Zip or Flex cars are parked near a work location and members (who can be some or all of your employees) have a card to access the car when necessary. Members use the cars when they need them, paying just a simple hourly rate that includes gas, insurance, and maintenance. It's far less expensive than owning and operating a car, and much more convenient than renting. This can provide peace of mind for employees who could feel abandoned or stranded without having their cars available. Of course, you will need to set up your own set of rules and restrictions regarding who can use the Flexcar or Zipcar and under what circumstances.

Section 10. Transportation, Travel, and Telecommuting

As is the case with most green initiatives, the company has to set the tone, provide encouragement, and get everyone onboard. One small business owner essentially held the morning meeting in the van as everyone rode to work. The result was a 9-to-4 day instead of 9-to-5, since one daily work hour was accommodated by the in-transit meetings. You need to sit down with your employees and work together on solutions, even if it begins as a two-day-a-week program. Remember, starting small will help you in your quest to become a more environmentally responsible business.

65 Create More Telecommuting Opportunities

It is estimated by several sources, including WorldatWork (an international nonprofit association of HR professionals), that some 30 million people work from home at least one day a month, with the number increasing steadily in recent years. The total number of full-time telecommuters, also called teleworkers, is now up to nearly 15 million and consistently rising.

The environmental benefits of telecommuting obviously begin with a reduction in highway congestion, which translates to a reduction in fuel emissions and pollutants. It also means a savings in energy and petroleum consumption. According to Elizabeth Rogers and Thomas Kostigen, co-authors of the *The Green Book*, the average commuter drives 10,000 miles per year, and all together, these commuters consume 67 billion gallons of gas. Along with saving billions of dollars in gasoline, as an employer, you can benefit by having fewer people in your office. This translates to using less equipment and saving on your electric bills. With more telecommuters, you can save on expansion costs, as well as office furniture and new equipment purchases. In fact, some businesses encourage workers to telecommute so they can downsize into a smaller facility.

Section 10. Transportation, Travel, and Telecommuting

Of course, making a shift to telecommuting won't work in all businesses. Hands-on employees in factories, retail staffers, and service providers still need to be physically present. Sales, customer services, marketing, research, IT, financial services, and accounting are listed among the leading positions where telecommuting has proven to be highly successful. It should also be noted that employees who are able to telecommute for some portion of their work week are typically less stressed and have a more favorable opinion of their employers. They also recognize the commitment to the environment made by the company and appreciate the flexibility of working from home.

Making the Move to Telecommuting

A shift to telecommuting means first determining which tasks can be done from a remote location. This means evaluating each job and considering what tools are required to perform the necessary tasks. Since nearly 70 percent of employees polled typically say they would like to work at home at least one day a week, you probably won't have much trouble convincing staffers to make the switch. However, you will need to establish policies in advance. These will include:

- **Guidelines:** You can set up an online file which outlines the expectations and responsibilities of teleworkers, so everyone is on the same page, so to speak. This should cover all potential concerns.
- **Communications:** There are several options widely available for communicating with your teleworkers, through either the internet or an intranet, using password-protected programs. However, for small businesses without highly sensitive materials, e-mailing documents back and forth can be effective.

  Cell phones and even landlines should also be utilized regularly. It is imperative that the lines of communication remain open and that employees and employers maintain a schedule for checking in and updating progress.
- **Accountability:** The major concern of employers and employees is that people working from home will be unproductive. Therefore, telecommuters need to be held accountable to

produce and complete x amount of work in x amount of time. Establish a list of measurable goals against which to determine the success of your teleworkers. Programs such as Norton PC Anywhere allow you to make work from an off-site location available to an on-site computer.

⊙ **Equipment:** Determine what your employees have and what they will need. Some businesses provide telecommuting equipment, but most do not need to, since almost everyone in the work force has computer capabilities at home. You need to make sure everyone has the capacity to communicate, which should be through a broadband connection rather than a dial-up. If you do need to provide equipment to someone, you can first look at on-site equipment that you are no longer using. Most offices have extra computers sitting around that can be upgraded and reused. Either way, you can then supply software as necessary and hook everyone up through the internet.

It should also be noted that along with the environmental benefits of telecommuting and the potential cost savings, you also broaden your horizons when it comes to hiring. Not only will the

INITIATIVES

Government initiatives are a good reason to consider telecommuting options.

Incentives for limited miles driven and no miles driven have been implemented in many states, starting with Maryland's "pay me not to drive" initiative. In parts of California, in and around Los Angeles, qualified employees can be eligible for a $500 tax credit if they telecommute or use other alternative work arrangements to reduce traffic congestion and subsequently improve air quality.

In Florida, the Department of Management Services has set up a statewide telecommuting program at **dms.myflorida.com**. Georgia, meanwhile, is working on a bill to provide state tax breaks to firms who let workers telecommute. Other states are working on bills to encourage telecommuting, so it is advisable to look at the latest legislation in your state.

concept of being able to work from home attract more potential employees, but you can expand your geographic field and hire from a much wider range of top talent, possibly even becoming global, while still remaining a small brick-and-mortar business.

Before jumping into a telecommuting setup, start with a trial period and determine if it is working efficiently for your business—perhaps two days a week for telecommuting. I worked at a website in the dot-com heyday that allowed us all to work from home one day a week. It worked very well and saved the company money on electric bills by having employees out of the office on various days. It also boosted morale and minimized commuting, while productivity remained the same.

While you can measure productivity and cost savings, you won't be able to measure the savings to the environment. However, by taking cars off the road, you are clearly making a dent in carbon dioxide emissions.

66 Think Greener Business Travel

The best way to travel green for business is to simply stay put and use teleconferencing or conference calls to put everyone in the same virtual office at the same time. The latest in technology allows you to handle such meetings from the comfort of your own office, complete with shared PowerPoint presentations, documents, and whiteboards, plus dazzling multiparty video and one-touch remote control to keep everyone up-to-the-minute in the same virtual meeting room.

Of course, there are those occasions where face-to-face meetings are far more effective and business travel is necessary. Obviously, for a short trip, such as going from New York to Washington, D.C., the train would be more energy- and cost-efficient than flying. Plus, by the time you got to and from the airport, not to mention through security, there would not be much of a time difference.

Buying carbon offsets or green tags to counterbalance your airline, train, or car travel is one step in the right direction. However, you can also green your trip. "We pulled all of the travel data together and identified the 10 cities that people travel to the most, and made a list of travel tips for those cities," explains Meghan O'Neill, editor of *Treehugger.com* and *Planetgreen.com*. From this information, Treehugger was able to provide essential green-friendly tips for each of those cities, including recommendations for greener hotels, transportation, and even restaurants. For example, rental car companies in some cities have hybrids available or you might not need a rental, but can simply use FlexCar or Zipcar for those times you need a vehicle. If possible, you can be booked in a hotel that is within walking distance of the meetings or the conference you will be attending. One earth-friendly traveler rents bikes in the various cities to which he travels.

O'Neill recommends that if you can't find greener alternatives, you should at least ask for them. "If, for example, more people ask for hybrid or low-emission rental cars, more rental companies will become aware of the public's interest, and in time they can make a change to accommodate this market," explains O'Neill.

While one individual traveler cannot make much of an impact, if each of the millions of business travelers each year took a few steps toward lowering the carbon footprint of his or her business trips, we could see a significant environmental impact. Therefore, it behooves business travelers or business trip planners to map out greener itineraries for each common travel destination.

You can also pick up a copy of the *Ethical Travel Guide* from Earthscan Publications and see if your destination is one of those included and what hints they may offer for greener travel.

For more on sustainable travel, you might take a look at **greenglobe.org** or **treehugger.com**.

67 Offset Business Travel With Green Tags

Yes, some business travel can be curbed through online technology, but face-to-face business and sales meetings are still integral to the success of many companies. While greener modes of transportation are excellent choices for local travel, you probably won't meet your deadline biking from New York City to Chicago for a seminar. The point is, travel is still a necessity for many businesses.

What you can do is offset some of the CO_2 emissions by purchasing green tags, which are not unlike carbon offsets, except that they are for travel purposes. In fact, you can make a point of utilizing travel agents and clubs who "get it" and make buying green tags easy. Green tags purchased to cover your airline travel are also called renewable energy certificates, and are a way of supporting new energy initiatives.

To provide a frame of context, a round trip from New York City to Chicago would produce roughly 1.5 tons of carbon dioxide per passenger! Bet you wish you could bike it now. A round trip from New York City to Los Angeles would product roughly three tons of carbon dioxide per passenger. By purchasing green energy tags from a reputable program, such as Trees For Travel (**treesfortravel.info**) or from Trees for the Future's Global Cooling Program, **treesftf.org/about/cooling.htm#travel**, you can help the planet by planting trees in increasingly barren areas where forests once stood. Since trees absorb carbon dioxide and produce oxygen, green tag purchases are essentially used to offset the effects of your company's business travel.

Of course, you need to have confidence that whoever is selling green tags will be using the money as intended. As with most businesses, there are some less than ethical characters out there. Look for tags endorsed by reputable authorities or certification services, such as a specific energy coalition or a government agency like the Natural Resources Defense Council. Ask for information, research the group or business, and make sure they are legitimate before you invest.

Clearly, green tags are not the sole answer to business travel. If you can cut down such travel, or take the train, or find an environmentally friendly way of getting from point A to point B, by all means do so. However, when you simply need to travel, consider green tags.

The hope is that, in time, new fuel and energy sources will substantially limit the CO_2 emissions from such travel. Then our propensity to destroy forests, pollute waterways, and perpetuate global warming will greatly diminish, removing the need to even buy green tags.

Intangibles

68 Change the Coffee Culture in Your Office

It is estimated that 55 percent of people over the age of 18 in the United States are daily coffee drinkers, which comes to roughly 110 million people. If this group drinks an average of three cups a day, that comes to 330 million cups per day, not including the occasional coffee drinkers. Therefore, if you can promote a "greener coffee culture," you can make a dent in the environmental woes and get your employees to continue thinking green.

First, opt for brewing in your company kitchen or wherever employees go (in-house) for snacks and/or beverages. Doing so allows your staffers to bring their own cups or mugs, rinse them out after drinking and reuse them, rather than getting and disposing of a Styrofoam or cardboard cup on a daily basis. It is estimated that by purchasing two cups of coffee a day in a disposable container, each person is contributing about 45 pounds of waste per year, or an additional 4,500 pounds for an office with 100 coffee drinkers.

If you insist on dropping by Starbucks, most will allow you to bring your own cup or mug. Some even offer a slight discount.

Next, opt for an energy-efficient (Energy Star) coffeemaker. Look for models that provide filterless brewing while using less energy. If you are in need of filters, you can buy durable, reusable stainless steel filters or those made from unbleached cotton to avoid tossing paper coffee filters into the trash numerous times a day.

You can also shop for a wide range of organically grown coffees, and try a few until you find one that suits the majority of tastes in your office.

If you are on the other side of the coffee equation and selling java is a part of your business, there are also a few things you can do besides using energy-efficient coffeemakers, recyclable filters, and so on. For one thing, you can encourage people to bring their own reusable cups by providing a discount. Perhaps every fifth or tenth cup is free, saving you money on purchasing Styrofoam or plastic cups. You can also look for recyclable stirrers, lids, and napkins.

Changing the coffee culture in your office or work environment will not result in significant environmental changes, but like many suggestions in this book, it will be an important part of the overall greener business mindset.

69 Quick Tip: Hold Greener Meetings

No longer do meetings require that everyone sit at a polished conference table that reeks of chemical cleaning compounds, in a cold, air-conditioned room designed to keep them awake, doodling on notepads while pretending to take notes.

The new greener meetings can take place in rooms with open windows for natural ventilation, laptops for note taking and sustainable wooden furnishings that require minimal cleaning with organic substances.

If meetings are scheduled at the right time of day and in the rooms with the largest windows, natural lighting can minimize the need for any other lighting. And if there is a need for snacks, fresh produce from local growers can be picked up and brought in by one of your staff in a reusable bag.

The point is, almost every aspect of the typical meeting can have a greener twist—even meetings held outside the office, where carpooling can take everyone from one location to the other, that is, if you don't find a healthy restaurant within walking distance.

Before the meeting, you can send out an electronic agenda and everyone can pull it up on their laptops, rather than having you hand out meeting agendas on paper. Yes, paperless meetings are possible and becoming more and more popular.

Environmental journalist Trish Riley also suggests looking for green facilities and places that are sensitive to your environmental wishes. "Some places even have electronic sensors that will turn off the lights and electricity when people are not in the room," adds Riley.

If you are in the position of planning and holding frequent meetings, review the components of your typical meeting, and see what you can make greener. Once you start the ball rolling, your attendees will likely have more suggestions.

70 Create a Green Team

One of the best ways to transition a business to be "environmentally proactive" is to establish a green team. With support and guidance by management, a green team can research and report on various means of improving sustainability within a company.

"Our green team was more of a bottom-up than a top-down effort," says Mark Parnes, Assistant General Counsel and green team member at the Palo Alto office of the law firm Wilson, Sonsini, Goodrich & Rosati. "A lot of employees were concerned (about the environment) and wanted to do something, so it was more a volunteer effort. Now we meet about every six to eight weeks as green team members to discuss ideas and possible company-wide initiatives," adds Parnes.

The key to a successful green team is utilizing members in their areas of expertise.

For example, whoever heads your production or facilities management might look into waste management alternatives, while your shipping department can research and present alternative shipping methods and your marketing department can consider greener means of marketing. In nearly every business, someone, typically

Section 11. Intangibles

the office manager, is in charge of office supplies, so he or she could be setting up a greener purchasing policy for such supplies.

Company-wide incentives can be put into place if participation is sluggish or enthusiasm is waning. Considering the growing interest in sustainability and green issues, most businesses of 50 people or more should not have a hard time pulling together a green team to meet monthly or bimonthly to discuss their findings and the potential for implementing greener strategies. One way to generate interest is to initiate a company-wide survey, which Parnes mentions as a means used by Wilson, Sonsini, Goodrich & Rosati, to see who wants to be a part of the team.

To start off, you will want to list the various departments that you would like included with a representative. An introductory meeting should take place, at which time everyone can list some common goals. Management should take part in the initial meeting to get the ball rolling, show support, and let it be known that there is room in the budget to make modifications—perhaps not every one suggested by the green team's findings, but at least a number of the recommended changes. At the initial meeting, you should:

- Make sure everyone knows one another.
- Appoint a leader.
- Appoint a secretary.
- Discuss overall goals, e.g., have a sustainability plan.
- Discuss finances.
- Discuss and list some general areas in which the company could become more sustainable; e.g., reducing waste, conserving energy and water, moving toward sustainable purchasing practices, using alternative means of transportation, etc.
- Discuss responsibilities of team members to research and report on their findings.
- Divide responsibilities so each member knows which area he or she will cover.
- Determine some rough deadlines for reporting on possible solutions.

- Develop a meeting schedule and determine a regular meeting place.
- Determine the best means of communication between members, which will typically be e-mail. However, you'll want to discuss whether periodic updates should be sent to everyone or held for meetings.
- Discuss any training that might be of benefit to the team, such as webinars, seminars, or books everyone should read.
- Finally, you will want to determine when the team or team leader will discuss the proposed changes with management, so they can be budgeted and brought to fruition.

Not only can a green team make a significant impact upon the environmental future of a company, but it can, and often does, serve as an excellent means of team building. Team members who are dedicated to environmental issues will also feel a much stronger commitment to the company when they take such an active role.

71 *Produce a Sustainability Report*

A sustainability report, not unlike a business plan, can serve a variety of functions. Also, like a business plan, it can change and grow with your company over time. By expressing in a document your commitment to sustainability, such a report can provide you with a roadmap illustrating where you have been and where you are planning to go as a more sustainable organization. By sharing such information about challenges and triumphs with your employees, stakeholders, and the public, you are building a commitment as well as keeping everyone abreast of your progress thus far. Additionally, a sustainability report is a good marketing tool, showing your greener side.

Section 11. Intangibles

"It's important not only to talk about what you're doing well and what you've accomplished, but also talk about what you're not doing well. That's a critical part of such a report," says Greg Owsley, Chief Branding Officer for New Belgium Brewery. "Consumers can see firsthand what you are doing, and they have so much more respect for you when you're willing to admit that you made a mistake or that you need to make specific changes," adds Owsley.

A sustainability report should establish your core values and include decision making principles that adhere to such values.

Within a sustainability report, you'll want to include:

- An overview of your business activities and business principles
- Your mission statement
- Your current energy needs and resources used
- An outline of your production process
- Your environmental strategies
- Your adherence to government regulations
- Your current sustainable use of raw materials
- Your current carbon footprint
- Life cycle analysis for your product(s), or cradle to cradle as it's sometimes called
- Upcoming plans and goals for the next 1, 3, and even 10 years
- How you plan to go about reaching your goals
- Current sustainability problems
- Means of addressing sustainability problems
- Your social and community activities
- Forthcoming initiatives within the community
- Risk management plans
- Charts, graphs, graphics, and any data to support and substantiate your plans

Often companies that write sustainability reports start by documenting the manner in which they are meeting environmental regulations. In some cases, this includes the specific tools used to meet regulations, such as more efficient product design.

Of course, one of the reasons you are in business (okay, the primary reason) is to make money. Therefore, you can, and should, show how your environmental policies fit into your profitability. Nobody expects you to sacrifice your profits to any significant degree in order to be more sustainable. You can, however, show shareholders and stakeholders how short-term expenses in areas such as eco-friendlier means of generating power (e.g., switching to wind turbines) will benefit the company's bottom line in the future.

In the end, the sustainability report should provide a realistic picture of how your business will address sustainability and profitability on a day-to-day basis. Finally, there are a variety of approaches that you can take to provide information in the sustainability report. First, it is not uncommon to acknowledge that your business is new at addressing ecological issues as a high-priority area of concern. Conversely, you may have been thinking and acting in a sustainable manner for years and only now are realizing the impact of your work. In this case, you can explain what you have been doing, possibly including specific examples, and add how you plan to continue. In some cases, you may tie your sustainability report into your annual report as one document for your shareholders. The bottom line is that you want to outline your sustainability efforts in an easy-to-read report that covers your efforts in the past and your goals for the future.

72 Hire a Director of Sustainability

Why not put someone in charge of the operation? There can be a sustainability officer, director of sustainability, or any other title that indicates the chosen individual has been selected to be the "green leader." Whether chosen internally or brought in from the outside, this individual needs to be enthusiastic about the subject at hand and eager to make a mark by studying the current status of all programs, processes, and products within the company. One of this person's first tasks will be to look for places where there is room for sustainable improvement.

Your green leader needs to address any and all areas pertinent to your business, including:

- Energy consumption
- Energy efficiency
- Product life cycles
- Manufacturing
- Shipping and distribution
- Production
- Packaging
- Sales
- Marketing and promotion
- Inventory
- Waste and waste management
- Safety and health issues

Of course, as is always the case in business, the financial bottom line needs to be an ongoing consideration in conjunction with efforts to make your company more sustainable. Cost-effective solutions are the ones that will matter most to your business, and plans or projects that are easy (and not costly) to implement will be the ones met with the most enthusiasm.

Your head of sustainability will need a fair degree of latitude to study and review the manner in which each department functions. Unlike an efficiency expert, he or she will most likely be welcomed into the company by the employees, many of whom are likely to be supportive of an overall environmentally friendly effort.

Communication is key to the success of a sustainability director, and with that in mind, he or she should be a skilled people person, able to listen effectively to your employees' concerns and be open to suggestions. Someone who can build a supportive framework and a team atmosphere is more likely to benefit your business than someone steeped in environmental jargon. Turning proposed changes and ideas into action will occur when everyone buys into the new mindset. This is especially true in the green context. Management also needs to show support for initiatives and recommendations brought about by whoever is in charge of this important area. This does not mean that all ideas will get the green thumbs-up and be launched, but the door needs to be open to acknowledging and discussing various environmentally intriguing ideas, which can range from simple things such as changing light bulbs and having desk-side recycling bins to more complicated plans for packaging redesign and incorporating renewable energy sources.

Finally, whether you find someone on a full-time or part-time basis or bring in a consultant, it's vital that he or she does not draw attention to upcoming plans or initiatives until those plans or initiatives are already enacted. Too many overly ambitious sustainability directors have promoted what they wanted to do before launching their plans. With green activist groups watching closely, you want someone at the helm who believes firmly that actions speak louder than words.

73 Establish a Consumer Recycling Program

You don't have to be a retailer to be a destination for consumers to bring products for recycling. Instead, you need to forge alliances with recycling centers and provide a location where consumers can drop off their old cell phones, printer cartridges, batteries, or other items. This is a good way to support a community-wide recycling effort while drawing people to your business.

Of course, depending on the industry you are in, you can build a reputation for recycling products in your business. A marvelous example is in the carpet manufacturing industry, where Carpet America Recovery Effort (CARE) has been established as a joint industry-government effort to increase the amount of recycling and reuse of post-consumer carpet in an effort to reduce the amount of carpet waste that ends up in landfills. You can visit them for more information at **carpetrecovery.org**.

In order to start a recycling drive, you need to determine where you can take the products that you collect for recycling, and what you can store in-house until it's time to drop off. A growing number of companies will take back products and in some cases, do their own in-house recycling. For example, a number of computer stores and manufacturers will rebuild with the parts from recycled computers. Patagonia takes back fleece and will recycle it into new products. In some cases, a business will actually make your product last longer, such as the folks at Denim Therapy, who will take back old jeans and even patch or reweave them for you. Even big box stores are getting into the act, as IKEA has a take-back program for CFL light bulbs and Office Max will take batteries, among other things.

Evaluate what you can collect and start a "take back" or consumer recycling program in your business.

Minimizing Tangible Goods

Another concept is to change the attitude of buyers when they're considering a purchase. As Meghan O'Neill of **Treehugger.com** explains, "Any time a company can think about dematerializing what they're selling and shift to a service mindset, they can start to reduce environmental impact." This concept can work with some products where actual material goods are not necessarily purchased, but products are either rented or transported electronically. Software companies can limit packaging and shipping by allowing you to buy their products electronically, via online downloads. Likewise, you can buy movies on demand through your local cable distributor without the actual movie being transported. The advent of rented and leased office furniture is also minimizing the need for more material goods to be produced. In short, if you can provide a service that limits the need for more new product production, you are also creating a form of recycling.

Of course, one of the pre-technology precursors of minimizing materialization was invented by Ben Franklin. If you guessed the library, you are correct. Yes, there are many books you will want to own, but if you took 20 percent of the books you read each year out of the library, you would save that much more paper used for printing books, not to mention the emissions from printing. An odd concept to mention in a book, isn't it?

In short, see if there are ways in which you can provide rentals, loans, leasing, electronic downloads, or other means of providing a service or product without always having to produce and transport a tangible item.

74 *Dress Greener*

While you cannot dictate what people will wear to work, you can establish casual Fridays and even lower the dress code so employees have greater flexibility in their choices. Doing so also makes it easier to control your heating and air conditioning as employees can dress to meet the seasonal changes.

If your business requires uniforms, then you can make more environmentally sound and socially responsible choices.

Cotton is typically thought to be one of the more environmentally friendly fabrics—at least more so than the many synthetic textiles made from fossil fuels. However, cotton growers use nearly one quarter of the world's insecticides while also using over 3,000 gallons of water per pound. Dyes and bleaches add toxins that end up in the ecosystem. Wool also requires many gallons of water per pound in the manufacturing process. Polyester, the most widely used manufactured fiber, is made from petroleum. The growing demand for man-made fibers, such as polyester, has nearly doubled in the last 15 years, according to figures from the Technical Textile Markets. Clearly, such an increase in manufacturing has had environmental implications. In short, petroleum-based products and the

Section 11. Intangibles

use of rayon in clothing manufacturing are destroying forests as well as proving harmful to the environment and to personal health. There is also the issue of socially responsible clothing manufacturing, meaning no sweatshop labor, no child labor, no animals killed. Therefore, you want to do some research regarding the process behind the manufacturing of clothing before you buy.

What can you wear, or ask employees to wear, that is environmentally friendly?

First, you can look for organic cotton, which is not treated with pesticides, herbicides, or insecticides during the growing cycle. Slowly but surely, such cotton growers are becoming more common. Look for labels that say "organic" or, if ordering uniforms, seek out vendors and uniform suppliers selling products made from organically grown cotton. You can also find organic wool, produced in accordance with federal standards, meaning that synthetic hormones or pesticides are not used on the sheep. In addition, chemical processes and dyes should not be used in the manufacturing process. Look for natural dyes, which are a better choice.

Another option is hemp, which is considered an environmentally friendly fabric made from plants that grow quickly and need little, if any, herbicides or artificial fertilizers.

Then there's bamboo. It has natural antibacterial properties and the fabric "breathes." As a result, the cloth is comfortable and biodegradable.

As clothing makers embrace eco-manufacturing processes, you will see more organic clothing choices that not only wear well, but are easy to clean.

Putting Your Best Foot Forward

75 *Use Green Marketing and Promotion*

Green marketing encompasses a twist on a familiar phrase. It's essentially "do as I do, not as I say." In essence, this refers to marketing green activities that are already being practiced rather than what you plan to do. Greenwashing, or claiming green behavior without demonstrating verified results, has created a "show me the green" attitude among both media pundits and consumers.

Green marketing may include anything from using recyclable paper and soy ink while reducing print output, to touting your renewable energy program, to working with community or statewide environmental programs.

There are three primary components to green marketing and promotion. They are:

1. Letting people know what you are doing to help benefit the planet
2. Marketing green products and services
3. Using green methods to achieve the first two

If, for example, you are using green in-house production methods to produce the greenest microwave, but promoting the new energy-saving device through high-gloss advertising and wiping out half a rainforest to cover your printing needs, you may be essentially defeating your own purposes. Therefore, green practices need to follow all the way through from production to packaging to sales to marketing, to the end user seeing the actual marketing materials and then recycling them. Sustainability is best as a corporate commitment. It starts from the top and continues from the supply chain through marketing and down to the consumers as the end recipients. "Consumers are driving all of this, because they want to buy from companies whose beliefs are most like their own," explains Duber-Smith, MS MBA and

Section 12. Putting Your Best Foot Forward

President of Green Marketing Inc. Therefore, you need to be practicing what you are marketing.

Since the American Marketing Association (AMA) held the first workshop on ecological marketing in 1975, a lot has happened and the market has grown to embrace eco-friendly marketing practices. The public has become savvier and has learned a lot about global warming and the planet's woes. "When we started, 11 years ago, we were helping some companies and government agencies with their environmental marketing. However, we would never have envisioned the explosion of interest that we've seen over the past 18 months," says Kevin Tuerff, president and co-founder of Enviromedia, a marketing firm in Austin, Texas (**enviromedia.com**).

What Can You Do?

First, before making any claims or promises, look closely at your own business practices. Along with the corporate leaders, such as Wal-Mart or Timberland, who have been trendsetting in recent years with their environmental initiatives, many small and midsize companies are taking the time and making a concerted effort to get their businesses in order before notifying the media who are chomping at the bit to get such stories. What are your sustainable practices? What is your carbon footprint? What kind of energy/power are you using in your business operations? What vendors and suppliers are you dealing with? Changing a few light bulbs won't fly, nor will buying carbon offset credits. Businesses are under much closer scrutiny today from eco-watch groups, so it is important that before you market yourself as green, you have made sufficient changes.

Next, look at your products and services. Can you create more environmentally friendly products? Packaging? Poland Spring water reduced the amount of plastic in their bottles and marketed that fact on their bottles. Whatever you are selling, you can typically find a greener way to produce it and package it. To be truly effective, go beyond government-required levels. Also, do the research, look back all the way and follow your products through the entire life cycle. If for example, you are a manufacturer of a sustainable, 100 percent, post-consumer recyclable product, but find that your suppliers are burning tons of fossil fuels to get the product to you or treating their employees in a socially irresponsible manner, then there is a glitch in the sustainable life cycle of the product and you will need to explore the situation more carefully before marketing your product as 100 percent sustainable.

Once you reach the point of having greener products (through the entire life cycle), and your business iis operating in a sustainable manner within cost-effective means, you can start letting the media know with electronic press releases and product samples. Word-of-mouth campaigns on the internet will also be beneficial, as will talking up sustainable practices (and showing examples) at seminars, conferences, and other speaking engagements in an effort to lead by example. Remember, word-of-mouth is a great low-cost, low-energy means of spreading the word.

Additionally, you will want to disclose content information and green practices used in creating, packaging, and shipping your products. Be sure that you are accurate in your claims. Again, ensure that you are not simply meeting requirements, but exceeding them.

Finally, you'll want to lend your support to community and industry efforts to meet sustainable energy goals. Sustainability is a universal concern, so becoming part of the larger community is beneficial and a cost-effective way to market your business in a green manner.

Of course, you need to be clear with what you are telling your potential customers. Since there are numerous definitions for what is considered a green business or green marketing, and different terms are used by every corporate marketing department and every media source, consumers are not necessarily sure what position your business is taking. Therefore, you need to make sure that you answer the basic marketing question, "How does this product or service benefit your consumer?" People want to know how the product is making their life greener and better. Even a very green product, packaged in an environmental manner, is of no use to someone unless there is a clear reason why the prospective buyer should purchase it. This is

WHAT IS GREENWASHING?

When a company falsely markets its activities as environmentally friendly, it is called greenwashing. Today, with more consumers putting pressure on companies to create greener programs, products and policies, many companies, rather than making a concerted effort, make promises they do not keep. Such greenwashing can be a PR nightmare for these businesses. In other cases, companies make sincere attempts, but do not achieve the greener presence they were hoping for. These are also lumped into the greenwashing category. In these cases, businesses should come clean about their efforts and acknowledge they miscalculated or simply went about the plan in the wrong manner. Honesty and transparency are the best means by which to respond to accusations of greenwashing. They should be followed with a sincere effort to rectify such environmental miscues.

especially true if you are asking the buyer to pay more for the greener benefits. Yes, you can focus on environmentally conscious, green consumers, but that is often preaching to the choir. Therefore, you will more likely want to extend your efforts to a mainstream market, many of whom are besieged by such marketing and need to know why they should believe you are truly green, unlike your greenwashing competitor.

In the end, making the message clear and simple and illustrating the benefits to your target audience can make green marketing efforts very effective.

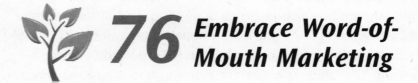

76 Embrace Word-of-Mouth Marketing

One of the best ways of reaching customers is through other customers. An unbiased testimonial or a simple "I loved that restaurant," or "That's a great store," from a friend will bring in customers or sell products without you having to lift a finger.

Section 12. Putting Your Best Foot Forward

There are many ways to start the ball rolling, especially on the internet, where one person can reach out to millions on a blog, in a chat room, on a discussion board, or through instant messaging with friends and family members. Encouraging this chain of communications is an inexpensive, environmentally friendly means of word-of-mouth marketing.

Many products, from Razor scooters to iPods, gained tremendous exposure from being seen by potential buyers. People saw the scooters and those white earbuds and started asking others where they got them. Providing product samples is another way to generate buzz by letting people see and experience a product before purchasing it. Free food samples in grocery stores have been a marvelous way of encouraging people to taste new products.

Public speaking presentations can also start the ball rolling. This can be anything from personal demonstrations of a product or service to an actual seminar. Look for public speaking opportunities to spread the word about what you offer.

The point is that word-of-mouth marketing is not only inexpensive, but it also uses fewer tangible goods, far less paper, and less energy than other forms of marketing, although it does require human energy. The idea is to empower individuals to share their viewpoints, which can be negative, if a product or service is substandard. Therefore, you need to work hard to make sure you are providing quality products and/or services. Viral marketing, or the means by which word spreads, has proven extremely effective in recent years. Businesses are just starting to recognize the power of such individual one-on-one promotion and harness it. This is largely due to the overabundance of traditional advertising and the need for consumers to differentiate among the glut of brands and products. After all, with a dozen brands of orange juice on the shelves, unless someone gives you a thumbs-up on one particular brand, it is hard to decide which one to buy.

For more on the benefits and power of utilizing word-of-mouth marketing, you can check out WOMMA, the Word of Mouth Marketing Association. WOMMA is made up of business leaders who are successfully pioneering word-of-mouth marketing techniques.

More information on the Word of Mouth Marketing Association can be found at **womma.org**.

77 Conduct Surveys to Gauge Your Customers' Interest in the Environment

A re your customers actively involved in environmental concerns? Are they recycling, biking to their jobs if possible, and supporting companies with sustainable practices? Are some of them still buying gas-guzzling cars or throwing away their old computers and cell phones? You need to determine where your customers stand on environmental issues, where you can satisfy their needs, and how you can gauge their concerns by conducting environmental surveys.

Whether you conduct a survey on your website, at your retail location, or via telephone, you need to get a pulse on your customers' degree of interest in and commitment to environmental concerns.

According to the 2007 Cone Consumer Environmental Survey, an impressive 93 percent of respondents believe that companies have a responsibility to help preserve the environment, while nearly 50 percent have purchased environmentally friendly products and more than one in five (21 percent) have donated to an environmental organization.

As is the case with any customer survey, you'll want to make your questions concise and easy to answer with either a multiple-choice or a short one- or two-word response.

In addition, you'll probably want to provide a simple incentive for taking the time to fill out your survey, which could be a 10 percent discount coupon, a free download (for an online survey), entry into a contest or some other low-cost perk.

Section 12. Putting Your Best Foot Forward

Keep in mind that when creating a survey, you do not want to ask for self-identifying information or respondents will shy away. For an online survey, you can ask for their e-mail addresses, but you need not get anything more. Then, while you may ask if they want to receive your newsletter or updates from your business, you should do nothing more with that e-mail address. Spam is another waste of energy and selling lists of e-mail addresses typically results in spam. In addition, you risk losing tremendous credibility if it becomes known that you do not preserve the privacy of the personal data (including email addresses) from your surveys.

You'll want to find out in what ways your customers are concerned about the environment and what actions they are taking. For example, do they recycle? Do they conserve energy? Do they conserve water? You can also make suggestions regarding products they can purchase to see if changes would be welcomed. For example, would they be apt to purchase products with minimal packaging? Would they buy a product or service from you if it were x percent costlier, but greener? Would they be interested in buying an inexpensive cloth bag they could use each time they frequented your store? By learning about customers' interests and their likely response to the greening of your business, you can determine which areas to change first and how rapidly you should proceed.

You will likely find that a large number of respondents will be very favorable about your greener changes. The key for you is to determine your priorities, since, like many businesses, you are limited by budgetary restraints as well as the practices of your suppliers. One major soda company found out the hard way that they should not have promised newer bottling before they checked to make sure their suppliers were onboard. Consumer groups were quick to call them on the carpet for their unfulfilled promises. Therefore, if there are areas in which you may not be able to make changes, you may not want to pose such questions until you know you can make the necessary adjustments.

Creating surveys and getting customer feedback is only part of the battle. You then need to review and analyze the responses to see what your customers want, and determine how to meet those requests. By engaging consumers and effectively responding to their environmental concerns with honest answers, you can help the environment while raising your bottom line.

78 *Quick Tip: Minimize the Media Blitz*

Clothing stores have video monitors playing while they pump in music on their elaborate sound systems. Meanwhile, restaurants have CNN playing on several TV monitors while you eat, and sports bars have not 3, but 17 games playing on big screens at once. Overkill? Indeed. Do your customers need an onslaught of media while they eat or shop? Even homebased business owners could probably stand a respite from that TV set on in the background seven hours a day.

The amount of energy used to produce this endless stream of media is exorbitant. While computers may be required for running your business, media for the sake of steady noise and so-called effect is unnecessary. Sports fans are now starting to complain that every break in the action need not be filled with the loud strains of rap, rock, or hip-hop. The propensity to constantly overwhelm the senses and eliminate any hint of quiet comes from a generation weaned on TV and videos—too much TV and too many videos.

Minimizing the media blitz is beginning to appeal to more and more people who simply want to go out for lunch without having every spare second filled with the endless scroll of headlines and sound bites. More people want to shop without feeling like they were suddenly dropped into a nightclub. More significantly, this ongoing media assault is wasting significant amounts of energy. If you own a store, a restaurant, or any such business in which you serve the public, you can do something positive for the environment by minimizing the endless media blitz and allowing people to once again resort to a couple of popular, old-fashioned activities: conversing and thinking. Remember, noise pollution is still pollution. So, in honor of the 1996 Broadway musical: *Take out da noise, Take out da funk.*

Locations, Locations, and Greener Locations

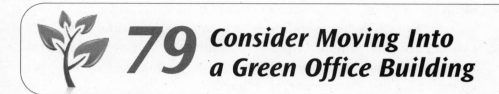

79 Consider Moving Into a Green Office Building

While contemplating how to green your business, why not seek out greener pastures? Many newly constructed buildings, and those being restored, refurbished, and renovated are being built with a concerted effort to go greener, not just because of the need to meet environmental standards, but in order to attract eco-minded tenants such as yourself. In fact, the United States Green Building Council (USGBC) rates and gives awards to the greenest buildings they can find. The USGBC Certification program, known as Leadership in Energy and Environmental Design, or LEED, was first established in 2000, and has since awarded certification to 715 buildings throughout the United States. With contractors and architects becoming more conscious of the demand for greener surroundings, there will certainly be more eco-friendly buildings on the way.

Of course, there is no single standard for an environmentally friendly building. Therefore, you'll want to look at what green features are offered before you embark on a relocation plan. Energy efficiency, waste management, and a clean, healthy work environment are among the primary criteria you should be seeking.

To get a better idea of what you may find when searching for a greener environment, here are some of the greenest buildings in America, and what they have done to put their stamp on sustainability.

The Phillip Merrill Environmental Center, owned by the Chesapeake Bay Foundation, is considered by some to be the world's greenest building. All materials in the building are recycled or created through processes that don't damage the environment. Rainwater is captured and reused for mopping and cleaning, thus limiting the amount of energy used to draw water from wells or other water systems. A controllable mechanical ventilation system provides fresh air in the building, while natural landscaping with native plants surrounds the facility. Temperature is monitored, and natural light and heating are used whenever possible. Materials such as cork, natural linoleum, bamboo flooring, and eco-friendly paints were all used in constructing the environmental center.

The Banner Bank Building in Boise, Idaho, owned by the Christensen Corporation, utilizes the surrounding seven acres to collect storm water, which is then reused in its sewage system. Backup generators run on biodiesel made from used vegetable oil.

The Conde Nast Building at 4 Times Square in New York City is 48 stories high, and although it was built a decade ago, it remains one of the greenest office buildings in the country. To maintain climate control without heating or air conditioning most of the year, the building was built with gas-fired absorption chillers, along with a high-performance insulating and shading curtain wall. A central air ventilation system was installed to provide fresh air, while recycling chutes were also included throughout the building.

The Bank of America Tower, also in New York City, at 1 Bryant Park, is a brand new 54-story green skyscraper with over two million square feet of high-rent office space. Raw materials used to build the 1,200-foot-high tower include mostly recyclable or reusable resources, and came from within a 500-mile radius to save on shipping demands. Rainwater and daylight are utilized in this highly sustainable building. LED signage, occupancy sensors, and fiber optics are all among the many eco-friendly lighting features; plus, the glass façade allows for plenty of daylight.

The San Francisco Civic Tower features integrated solar panels for energy, chilled ceilings, a raised floor ventilation system, and greenhouses on every floor.

The Clinton Presidential Library in Little Rock, Arkansas demonstrates that not only office buildings go green. The renovated building includes more recycling options and a rooftop garden to absorb carbon, reduce rainwater runoff, and regulate temperatures.

If You Can't Find a Green Building ...

Since many older buildings are not up to the same green standards as their newer neighbors, you will want to assess whether or not the building you are considering is being run and maintained in a green manner. Therefore, if you are moving into an office building, or even a retail space, managed by a management company, or a landlord, you might want to inquire about:

○ The HVAC system. How old is it? Is it routinely maintained? Are there separate zone control thermostats?

○ Are Energy Star or similar appliances already in place and if not, can you replace the current ones?

○ Is building debris recycled or carted off to landfills?

○ Is the building up-to-date on asbestos removal, lead paint exposure, and have all unsafe materials been removed?

○ Are architectural materials such as doors, partitions, old cabinets, blinds, carpets, windows, wiring, receptacles, equipment, and fixtures typically reused if possible or recycled if not reusable?

○ Are there procedures in place for monitoring, inspecting, maintaining, and operating all equipment that can affect energy consumption? Is air quality also monitored?

○ How often is the insulation (on wiring and pipes) inspected and maintained?

○ What other green procedures are in place or are being planned for the facility?

○ Can you install environmentally friendlier appliances such as lighting, ceiling fans, and other accoutrements?

For the most part, it's usually not too difficult to determine from the onset whether the landlord or building owners get it or not. A general question about how environmentally sound the building is will elicit either a list of eco-friendly procedures and plans for the future or a dumbfounded "Huh?"

There are also some basics you can look for on your own. For example, is the building getting direct sunlight or is it blocked by surrounding buildings? Is it feasible to bike to work, or would you be situated between major highways? Is there acreage for planting and growing, or is there pavement as far as the eye can see? Do you see recycling bins or dumpsters?

Does the air inside the building seem clean and fresh or stale and musty? You can make a building, or at least your portion of it, greener by taking actions in line with your sustainability objectives.

80 Expanding Your Facility? Build Green!

While it may be several years down the road before you will even consider adding on to your current facility, when the time comes, you should strongly consider sustainable building practices and materials. Green building can minimize your long-term maintenance costs by maximizing your energy savings. In addition, along with the many environmental benefits, your new green addition or new facility will benefit your employees' health as well as serve as a model of sustainability in your community and within your industry. As environmental architects and engineers become easier to find, you will want to discuss the possibilities of a greener environment before you plan your expansion.

The key to green building is to determine ways to conserve the natural resources of the earth by means of efficient use of energy, building materials, and water. The goal is to provide a healthy atmosphere for employees and for the surrounding community, one that has little to no carbon imprint. If possible, your new location or addition should also have as minimal an impact as possible on local energy resources.

Most green building today is achieved through an integrated process that begins during the pre-design phase. New structures are typically seen as whole buildings from the start, since the systems and components are integrated. The process is known as "whole building design" and the entire building acts as one unitary system. Of course, if you are adding on to your existing structure, your architect will have to determine how you can integrate your current energy system with that of your new space. This may mean upgrading to a greener energy source (such as renewable energy) across the board, if possible. In fact, expansion may be the perfect time to implement greener practices for your entire facility.

The goals of green building include:

- Energy efficiency, which means minimizing traditional energy use while providing the same benefits and comforts.
- Water efficiency, which can include reusing water, collecting rainwater, and so on.
- Improved indoor air quality. This is a broad term that can include anything from nontoxic paints and chemicals to eco-friendly flooring, as well as good ventilation.
- Utilizing the land in an efficient manner, which can include landscaping, bicycle paths, environmentally friendly non-asphalt parking lots, and more.
- The use of green building materials should also be a key factor when planning your expansion.

Renewable, recyclable, and environmentally responsible materials are what you are seeking when planning to build green. In addition, you'll want nontoxic materials with minimal, if any, chemical emissions, also known as having low Volatile Organic Compounds (VOCs). You will also want materials that do not require toxic or VOC-producing chemicals for their production. An architect who is knowledgeable and experienced in sustainable building will advise you regarding the best materials, and walk you through a life cycle assessment. Of course, this will depend in part on the size and scope of your expansion and where you are located. Along with recycled materials, you will find that there are certified woods and various organic products that can be used in the building process, many of which are available locally, thus minimizing the need to import materials from long distances. Many green builders are able to find local reusable materials, such as wood salvaged from old barns, which is becoming more widely used in some areas of the country.

The United States Green Building Council (USGBC) is one place to find out more about Leadership in Energy and Environmental Design (LEED), which is a Green Building Rating System®. You'll find them at **usgbc.org**.

You may also want to visit the American Institute of Architects site at **aia.org** or the Sustainable Building sourcebook at **greenbuilder.com/sourcebook**.

81 *Moving Part II: Consider a Brownfield*

While this will not be an option for most businesses, it will affect those, particularly in manufacturing, that are planning to move or to expand their businesses significantly in the near future or down the road.

One of the most energy-efficient, cost-effective means of moving is to purchase a brownfield as your new location. Brownfields are polluted locations, typically factories, warehouses, old gas stations, or railroad stations that have been abandoned. The U.S. EPA defines a brownfield as "Real property, the expansion, redevelopment, or reuse of which may be complicated by the presence or potential presence of a hazardous substance, pollutant, or contaminant." When economic difficulties cause factories to close, the locations may end up as brownfields. In other instances, businesses could not afford to comply with new environmental laws and statutes and simply abandoned their facilities.

Once upon a time, if you walked by such an abandoned building, you would have continued walking. Today, thanks to new technology and brownfield redevelopment specialists, these old, abandoned eyesores can become new and profitable homes for business.

Redeveloping and breathing new life into these old, often contaminated, structures or tracts of land has proven very profitable for companies that would prefer to clean up an old structure rather than build a brand-new one from scratch. On behalf of the environment, we thank you. New construction is one of the leading causes of carbon emissions, toxins released into the environment, and subsequent pollution, not to mention the massive amounts of waste and potential for personal injury.

Redevelopment of a brownfield can:

- Use the land in a more productive manner that will serve the environment.
- Create new jobs.
- Increase area property values.
- Eliminate the need for a typically lengthy building process.
- Eliminate dangerous, potentially unsafe, and often unsightly structures that are harmful to the ecosystem of an area.
- Help maintain and conserve rural areas and grasslands where new buildings and structures might otherwise be built.

The concept of finding and transforming a brownfield site into a usable facility for your business is called sustainable brownfield regeneration. This refers to the management, rehabilitation, and reuse of the facility in a manner that is environmentally sound and economically viable for a business.

Currently, it is estimated that there are more than 400,000 such sites in the United States (across all states); most of these sites are undervalued. Many have contamination in underground pipes or storage areas that are not obvious upon first inspection.

Today, with land becoming less available in highly populated areas, you might decide to inquire about the costs of renovating and utilizing a brownfield. Before a brownfield can be cleaned up and revitalized, environmental studies and tests need to be conducted. Thanks to increasingly sophisticated technology, this has become an easier task than in the past, which allows more business owners to seriously consider cleaning up and utilizing these buildings.

However, technology notwithstanding, there can be some difficulties getting such a project started. "A lot of times, finding the per-

Section 13. Locations, Locations, and Greener Locations

son who owns the property can be difficult, and there may be 'cloudy' titles, judgments, and foreclosures. You'll need to deal with the third parties to clear the title," explains Robert Colangelo, CEO of the National Brownfield Association and publisher of the bi-monthly publication *Brownfield News*.

"The first place to start is the local government department of records, or the planning board, to try and find the rightful owners of the property," adds Colangelo. In some instances, ownership may be in the hands of the state. In addition, you will find that state and local governments have their own rules, regulations, and interpretations in place. Should you be able to contact the owners, you can then find out if they are willing to sell the property. If they are, you will first want to have a thorough inspection and detailed evaluation of the property done by engineers experienced at working with brownfields. Bringing in a consultant can help you evaluate what needs to be done, and know which engineers will need to inspect and write reports on the property. This may include civil, chemical, soil, geo-technical, and other engineers, as well as specialists in specific areas. The National Brownfield Association, **brownfieldassociation.org**, can be an excellent source when looking for experts and consultants in your area to guide you through the process.

Many states, as well as the federal government, have programs in place to help you in redeveloping brownfields, should you find one that the owners are willing to sell to you. Of course, the costs involved to complete the work need to be feasible. In some cases, the cost to clean up a facility may be prohibitive, while in other instances, you will find that with a little effort you can get the job done at a reasonable rate, even if that means getting some volunteer help.

The next time you see an abandoned building, keep in mind that it may represent a second life waiting to be uncovered and reused.

82 *Maintain Some Green Acreage*

Pangea Organics actually has a 3,000-square-foot vegetable garden that is operated by the employees and can feed the whole staff seven months out of the year. Music Today, a company in Crozet, Virginia, has an on-grounds employee garden where everyone can get their hands dirty while greening their own work environment. Meanwhile, a Subaru plant in Indiana has an area designated as a wildlife habitat. In short, many businesses are no longer paving paradise to put up a parking lot, as Joni Mitchell once sang.

Instead, maintaining green-lands has become a growing trend among environmentally conscious businesses. Whether you are providing an oasis for local wildlife or growing native varieties of plants, you can breathe new life into your surroundings by maintaining some green acreage. You can also practice xeriscaping (a marvelous word for Scrabble players), which is the practice of landscaping with slow-growing, drought-tolerant plants. Your company land can be maintained by employees and the community. In fact, it can serve as a focal point or gathering spot. "We have bike-in movies," says Greg Owsley of New Belgium Brewery, which takes the old premise of drive-in movies and applies it to having people show up on bicycles to watch a film outdoors. The point is that land can be used in a wide variety of ways, whether it's growing products used in your manufacturing or bringing the community together in a show of green awareness.

In urban areas, as mentioned elsewhere, roof gardens have been built atop many high-rise buildings, designed in conjunction with architects and urban landscapers to create "cool" roofs.

Even parking lots can be greener. "You can create parking lots that have permeable surfaces instead of just asphalt," explains Meghan O'Neill of **Treehugger.com**, referring to alternatives such as using paving stones where water can actually seep into the ground. An example of an eco-friendly parking lot is one built recently in Williamsburg, Virginia, at the Prime Outlets shopping mall. Built with environmentally friendly materials, the porous concrete is designed to allow water to pass through it while still serving as a flat parking surface. The water, which could become contaminated from oil or other chemicals on the lot's surface, is filtered into groundwater supplies, rather than running off into nearby streams as it would do with asphalt. In this case, the water is filtered and then reused to irrigate trees and the landscape around the lot itself.

The point is, your land, from green spaces to parking areas, can all be eco-friendly if you stop to take time to "smell the flowers" rather than the asphalt.

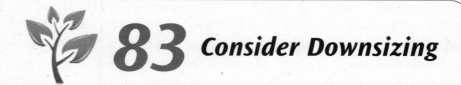

83 *Consider Downsizing*

Bigger is no longer necessarily better. While large-screen TVs are in vogue, smaller cars, cell phones, and cameras have certainly come of age. And, for businesses with excessive space, it may also be time to downsize, especially in a struggling economy. Downsizing can be a tremendous cost saver when it comes to paying rent. It can also save you a significant amount of money on energy, and as a result, be a big plus for your profit margin. After all, why spend all that money heating or air conditioning a huge space when you can control the temperature in a smaller space through passive solar heating? The increase in telecommuting and videoconferencing has minimized the need for large office spaces and expansive conference rooms. Flex schedules also allow for space sharing in some offices, especially if employees are using laptops that allow each person to bring his or her computer to a shared workstation.

Look around and determine if you are fully utilizing your space or if downsizing would be an alternative. In some instances, businesses have opted to share space and even share equipment, such as a copy machine or office supplies. Consider the needs of your business and whether you could do just as well in less space, utilizing the money you save to promote your products and/or services. There are many businesses already doing big things from small locations.

Downsizing is not only for offices. Even retailers can benefit from smaller locations.

Nau Inc., the environmentally friendly outdoor apparel company based in Portland, Oregon, has opened 2,000-square-foot outdoor apparel stores in their home state and in a few other locations around the country. These stores contain limited inventory and plenty of computer kiosks where customers can research and order products directly from the company's website while shopping in the store. The idea is to offer the best of both worlds. With Nau's limited inventory, customers can see, feel, and try on items (which are made of recycled materials) and also utilize technology. Shoppers can see the full range of options at the computer kiosks and have their selections shipped from a central warehouse directly to their homes.

Nike, Adidas, and Patagonia are among the other companies that have opted for smaller high-tech stores, which save them money on shipping inventory as well as on energy usage. Store kiosks use less energy than heating, cooling, and lighting a larger shop. Thinking smaller can benefit the planet and your bottom line.

Social Responsibility and Doing Better for Your People

84 Start a Program of Company-Wide Volunteer Hours

Yes, it's very easy to write a check on behalf of your company to benefit a cause or community organization. However, it's far more beneficial on many levels to start a program where employees volunteer a certain number of hours each month on company time to an organization of their choosing. You may want to determine that this will not include religious and political groups to avoid any potential misunderstandings.

One such community service program was set up back in 2001 by the folks at Clif Bar, the California-based energy and protein bar manufacturers. "We called it the 2080 Program, since that's the number of hours people typically work in a year," explains Kate Torgerson, head of Clif Bar Public Relations. Employees were able to volunteer with pay for several hours per week.

Clif Bar also organized an event of their own, which included picking up trash on a nearby beach. "One of the leaders of our R&D department was so affected by picking up all of the plastic and Styrofoam waste that when he received packages with Styrofoam peanuts, he wrote back to the companies politely explaining why he would appreciate it if they would send future packaging without this plastic or Styrofoam, explaining how it affects wildlife," explains Clif Bar staff ecologist Elysa Hammond. The result was far less plastic included in packaging. The point is such a project can enlighten members of your own staff in ways that make them feel compelled to share with others. It's not uncommon to learn a lot more from being in the throes of an activity than from simply reading about it.

Timberland is another example of a company that recognizes the value of inspired employees. With that in mind, they allow 40 hours per year—while on the clock—for each employee to do volunteer work.

Additionally, such company-wide volunteer programs work on various other levels. For example:

- ✪ **The Company Sets the Tone:** What better way to show employees a company-wide commitment than putting your money where your mouth is? If they are still on the clock while volunteering, then you must be committed to making changes in the environment and in the greater community.

- ✪ **It's Great Team Building:** People feel a greater sense of togetherness picking up trash on a beach or teaching children about recycling than they typically do while toiling away at the office.

- ✪ **It's Terrific Public Relations:** Wear those company T-shirts and show everyone who passes by that your company is doing as much good outside the office walls as inside.

- ✪ **Benefiting the Community:** Businesses that support their communities find that communities support them as well.

In the end, such efforts pay for themselves with less employee turnover, greater motivation, a positive image in the community, and a positive impact on the environment.

As Clif Bar has discovered, this is a win-win-win-win situation.

85 Support and Sponsor Environmental Groups and Causes

Supporting and sponsoring green activities, programs, and forthcoming events can serve a variety of functions for your company. First and foremost, you are helping the planet. You are, however, also providing an excellent opportunity for your employees to embrace your involvement in such efforts while presenting your company to the public in a greener light. In addition, such activities typically support health and, in many cases, exercise and athletics. Many companies are joining in and aligning themselves with such eco-friendly initiatives.

Clif Bar & Company sponsors over 2,000 athletes in a wide variety of sports and outdoor activities from mountain climbing to triathlons to bike races and more. In addition, their Two Mile Challenge was designed to promote bike riding as an alternative means of transportation. Clif Bar & Company has also taken part in working with Habitat for Humanity and teamed with the Breast Cancer Fund on a variety of programs and events that have raised over $1.5 million dollars. All told, the health bar company has supported 90+ nonprofit organizations, many of which are focused on the betterment of the planet, while others support health and education-related issues.

While you may not find yourself supporting as many projects and organizations as Clif Bar, you can very easily start looking around for programs to support. Start by seeking potential partnerships and programs at a local level. In fact, you might spread the word around the company by asking everyone to look for such programs and see what they find. Set up a suggestion box where employees can write down the names of organizations with whom you could partner. By browsing local newspapers, talking to city or county officials, surfing the internet, or finding a community calendar of activities from a reputable source, you can easily find out what eco-friendly groups are active in your area. Believe me, as environmental programs grow in prominence, you should not have trouble finding such organizations with which to align.

If your business is small, you can have a company-wide meeting to determine which of these groups you'd like to work with. In a larger group situation, you could ask for representatives from various departments to help make the decision. As is usually the case, the more people that get onboard early, the greater the ownership and subsequent participation in forthcoming activities. Of course, you will also need to decide what your level of participation will be. In some cases, you will be donating money. For example, 1% for the Planet is a nonprofit organization comprised of companies that have pledged 1 percent of their annual profits to environmental causes. Both Clif Bar and New Belgium Brewery are among over 600 companies that have signed up as members, which can now be found in some 20 countries (**onepercentfortheplanet.org**).

The other alternative is to get involved by participating. Ideally, it's nice to have a mixture, where you donate to causes while also participating in grassroots activities. This could mean anything from a race to raise money or educational activities to raise awareness to a hands-on cleanup of a local park.

Before pledging to contribute to or work with any group or organization, check out their credibility. Unfortunately, there are a few groups (fortunately, not many) that are either bogus or well intentioned but not yet well organized. Look for their status as a nonprofit in the community.

Another option is to raise money as a company through your own activities and team up to make a donation to a chosen environmental group whose work reflects what you believe. Discuss the many options and determine which group (or groups) you would like to support. Under the federal tax code, regular deductions as contributions from your employees' salaries (before taxes) can be made and sent to an organization with nonprofit status.

The key to a successful partnership is bringing something to the equation, whether it's manpower, money, beer, or all three as in the case of New Belgium Brewery. You can then learn from what your partners bring in terms of expertise. Partnering is a two-way street,

ENCOURAGE PHILANTHROPY

You can support your employees by encouraging them to seek out and get involved in philanthropic initiatives and then provide company backing and/or support. Encouraging your employees to recommend and drive philanthropic ventures can result in happier employees and a more positive relationship with your community.

and communications must be strong and respectful from the beginning. Such activities are not designed for PR purposes: they are for the environment. If you get PR from your efforts, it can be a plus, as you can spread the word about sustainability and worthy causes, but don't enter into such alliances with camera crews at the ready.

86 Become a Role Model: Educate Others on Sustainability

The folks at New Belgium Brewery take great pride in the fact that the vice president of sustainability from Wal-Mart toured their facility and spent a long time asking questions, picking their brains and reviewing what they saw. The brewery is among several businesses that are now serving as role models for others to follow. "The best way is to focus on what we're doing as a company and allow other industry people to talk about it," says Greg Owsley of New Belgium. Owlsley attended a confab of sorts with Ben & Jerry's, Patagonia, Hewlett-Packard, Nike, and other businesses to discuss how to be more sustainable and how to further their sustainability output.

It's not hard today to find conferences, seminars, and workshops that focus on corporate sustainability. You can look online for upcoming events, many of which are sponsored by universities. There are some you may wish to attend, and others where you may want to present, depending on where you are in your sustainability efforts. Success breeds success, especially in an area such as sustainability, where many business owners are hesitant to jump in with both feet. Most business owners today are aware that they should do something; they just don't know what it is. Therefore, once you have made your way around the learning curve, you can educate others on how you got there and what successes and failures you've had along the way. Likewise, you can continue to learn from those who implemented sustainable practices prior to your company's involvement.

You can also meet with other businesses in your community to discuss sustainability issues, exchange ideas, and work together to educate the public at large. A growing number of businesses have taken the message outside corporate circles to schools to educate students at all grade levels about what can be done to help the troubled planet.

Arranging and running seminars in your community can be a way to enlighten the public and establish a closer bond with potential and current clients or customers. If you are a manufacturing company, tours of your facility are also a marvelous way to illustrate what you are doing environmentally.

Being a sustainable role model means leading by example and sharing your knowledge and activities with businesses and the public at large.

SPREAD THE WORD

Spreading the word is part of being green. However, you can also work with your suppliers to help them develop sound environmental practices. Starbucks, for example, pays their coffee farmers prices for beans that are above the going rate, while also working with them to use the most environmentally friendly methods of growing and harvesting the coffee beans.

By teaming up with your suppliers, you form a stronger bond that can benefit all three components of your bottom line: environmental, social responsibility, and financial.

87 *Become the Green Center for Your Community*

It is particularly advantageous for retailers to become the green center of their community, since it is a good way to:

○ Attract more customers and increase profits, since green is the color of choice today

○ Provide practical information to the public

○ Make an impact through sharing your newfound knowledge

There are a variety of green mapmakers today that provide information on anything from local farmers in a specific region to green businesses and nature areas. Go to **greenmap.org** to get more information on green mapping.

For your purposes, however, you need not necessarily create a green map of your local area (although it is a possibility). Instead, you can become the one-stop location where customers and visitors can find out about activities, organizations, businesses (like yours), and recreational opportunities that all have a green tone. For example, is there an upcoming 10-mile run to raise money to clean up a nearby waterway? Are there business owners who utilize only green materials? Are there organic businesses nearby? Is there a nearby hotel that is known for using sustainable energy? Are there local farms from which to buy fresh, organic foods?

Your green community center can be a source for all such green information. From a simple bulletin board to a host of listings printed on recyclable paper to an active information booth with a host during certain hours, you can provide a wealth of green resources. In a small town, you can cover specifics, while in a larger urban market, you may include many of the dedicated green organizations and their contact information, as well as listing community activities and events. Once word spreads that you are the green center of the community, other businesses and organizations will supply you with information on what they are doing to benefit the environment.

If you have the available space, or can utilize nearby space at a reasonable cost, you can also have a series of green-topic lectures on sustainability and let people know what they can do at an individual level or through their businesses.

Sharing your knowledge with the community is a marvelous way to encourage and promote greater environmental awareness and community participation. Of course, this is more effective if your visitors can see that you are practicing what you preach by operating in a sustainable environment.

88 *Produce a Green Newsletter*

Clif Bar's newsletter is packed with information about their sustainability efforts, their involvement in the community, and employees who are making exceptional efforts to change the environment.

You, too, can spread the word, not simply as a means of touting your accomplishments, but as a means of encouraging your customers, clients, suppliers, vendors, and neighbors to get involved.

Whether you use post-consumer recycled paper for hard copies that can then be recycled again, or go electronic with an online newsletter, or both, a newsletter can be a great resource for disseminating information on your own green initiatives, greener products, and overall sustainability practices, as well what's going on in your community.

Perhaps a look at EPA's new consumer newsletter, *GO GREEN!*, will inspire you. The EPA newsletter includes information about activities and events and enviro-tips on ways to better the environment at a practical, hands-on level.

As an entrepreneur, you can also use your newsletter for marketing and promotion, since you are still a business. People will be receptive as long as you are promoting green products and sustainability. Use the area around your primary content to promote your products or services. In addition, make your newsletter viral, so readers can easily forward articles, green tips, or even the entire newsletter to a friend. This builds your readership and spreads the word about the environment and your business. Remember, however, only send your newsletter to a permission-based list, which you can generate at your business, from your website, and from your marketing efforts and materials.

A monthly or even bimonthly newsletter does not have to be long. You want to include just enough content to keep readers interested, especially with material that pertains to them and things they can do. You might even elect to feature stories, letters, and/or photos from customers about their own green practices at home or at work. There are plenty of options, but a newsletter that is informative, easy to read, and touches on the environmental concerns of many is an excellent means of providing information while marketing yourself as a greener business.

89 *Lobby for Green*

You can either wait for legislation favoring environmental concerns or you can get involved and try to expedite the process. By lobbying for green legislation, you put yourself in a position of taking a stand and potentially making a positive impact on your community. Of course, before you can take a stand on environmental issues regarding regulation and legislation, you have to:

○ Make sure you have your house in order, meaning you need to be practicing what you are preaching.

○ Understand the pending regulations and legislation and exactly what they entail. This means doing your homework and determining if you want to take a position on a specific issue or not.

Section 14. Social Responsibilty and Doing Better for Your People

♻ Know the proper channels through which you can communicate with your government representatives.

The Clean Air Act and Clean Water Act are examples of government bills that were passed in an effort to protect the environment. However, these are just the tip of a major iceberg that requires more stringent guidelines and stricter enforcement as new technology outpaces new laws and governance.

The hope is that the federal government will take greater steps to control and minimize the amount of pollutants and greenhouse gasses produced by the (numerous) companies that are barely complying with the current standards.

As a business owner, you can not only support federal bills designed to improve the current environmental policies, but also drum up local support by explaining such legislation to your employees, suppliers, vendors, and customers. Along with showing support for your local congressional leaders, you can build greater support by creating public awareness of issues that need to be addressed sooner rather than later.

Numerous large companies are members of the United States Climate Action Partnership, including Ford, GE, the NRDC, and DuPont. Your company can also be part of such joint ventures at a national or local level. Working with other companies can increase your visibility as an environmental leader.

In many towns and neighborhoods, small businesses have teamed up to promote and support legislation to clean up local waterways, protect wildlife, or enforce stricter regulations regarding anything from auto emissions to trash removal. Starting such a campaign means setting aside time to research issues of concern to your business and the community, clearly defining your position, understanding the political process, and then reaching out to the appropriate parties, including the lawmakers, the media, and the public at large.

Today, with so many advocacy groups focusing on environmental issues and concerns, it is very likely that you will not have to go it alone. In almost any city, town, or community, you will find like-minded individuals and businesses already involved in the fight for greater government involvement and stricter environmental regulations. You can also find green industry associations that you can join. This way you can have a more powerful voice.

Since pollution, global warming, greenhouse gas emissions, and other means of destroying the planet have had such a head start, you can be sure that enacting climate change and eco-friendly legislation (and enforcing it) will be a long-term battle. The sooner you start lobbying, the better.

90 Attract Green Employees

Look for employees who share your vision. In today's eco-minded environment, that should not be too difficult.

"Dedicated to selling only sustainable wood products, we have a core mission that has to do with sustainable forestry and ecosystems," explains Lewis Buchner, CEO of EcoTimber, a leading supplier of eco-friendly flooring. "We get some very talented and high-caliber employees. If it weren't for our environmental mission, they probably wouldn't have any interest in working for a wood products company," adds Buchner.

As a green company, you will be in a far better position to attract top talent. While this is not a reason for going green, it is a benefit that comes with becoming part of the solution and not the problem. A largely social and environmentally conscious generation of students are coming into the work force, while others are already there. In fact, according to a survey conducted by Monster Trak in late 2007, college graduates are looking to work for businesses that help the environment. The survey showed that as many as 80 percent of those surveyed were interested in a job that has a positive impact on the environment, and 92 percent would choose working for an environmentally friendly company. Some employees responded that they would work for less money if it meant being part of a more environmentally and socially conscious organization. A 2006 survey by progressive community network Care2 showed that almost 50 percent of employees polled would accept lower pay to work for a socially responsible company. Also, according to the survey, 40 percent of employees would be willing to work longer hours for a job at a socially responsible company.

You set out to find individuals interested in bettering the environment by posting information about your eco-friendly philosophy on the job posting boards, many of which now include environmental or green job listings as a specific category. Employers who are making their own environmentally positive attitudes known in job recruiting are already finding an increase in respondents, many of whom, as Buchner alluded, might not have otherwise applied. You can, therefore, attract the best prospects, which in turn can help you surge forward into the future with the sustainable goals that you have set forth to achieve.

Of course, just as there is greenwashing, there is also greening a resume. Therefore, you will want to do some follow-up so you do not attract employees looking to jump on the green bandwagon. Conversely, well intentioned, dynamic individuals with great passion for the environment will still need to possess the skills you require and not have misdirected passion. After all, you are still running a business.

By and large, being a truly green business will attract a larger group of like-minded and top-level candidates.

91 Treat Your Employees to Wellness

When I worked at **Sites.com** in Brooklyn, New York during the dot-com craze of 2000, we had yoga classes twice a week in our office, run by a licensed yoga instructor, complete with mats and everything. Although I was not a yoga enthusiast, it was a stress-reducing benefit to some of the executives and other staffers.

While wellness is not necessarily green, the concept of social responsibility to your staffers is part of the overall green equation. Health and wellness of body and mind go hand in hand with concerns for a healthy global picture. Healthy, unstressed employees are a benefit to your company, and by creating an atmosphere of good-will and providing health services, you are empowering your people to take on larger, more global responsibilities. Wellness today can take on a number of forms, and businesses are looking at positive returns brought about by offering various health-related services, events, and activities.

Major companies like AXA Financial feature entire wellness fairs once or twice annually, and provide full medical screenings for employees. For many smaller and midsize companies, however, selecting a variety of affordable health and wellness offerings, from lectures to hands-on activities, can be very beneficial. Of course, health and wellness should not be an occasional concern, but an ongoing aspect of your HR programs. Bringing in an expert consultant in wellness training and management can help you determine an ongoing plan that will benefit your company in the long run. Key areas of focus, including staff turnover, low morale, absenteeism, employee fatigue, and physical concerns, can all be addressed and improved with a well constructed plan. You can also reduce your health-care expenses by taking a proactive wellness stance.

A new company called The Wellness Track, **thewellnesstrack.org**,

PROMOTE WELLNESS DAYS PROPERLY

Medical screenings, chair massages, and lectures on anything from diet and nutrition to HIV can all be very beneficial as part of a wellness day or a special seminar. However, you need to make it clear from the start that such activities, while part of the workplace, are also separate from the workplace. In other words, your employees' medical information will not be shared with anyone in your office. They should not feel embarrassed or like they are being judged if they attend a workshop or seminar. They are also not being considered absent or avoiding work, as this is specifically provided as a benefit, a positive one. Promote wellness days and activities as a win-win situation for everyone with no negative repercussions from you as an employer.

is an example of a small independently launched company designed to help employers keep their employees healthy—and smiling! The Wellness Track offers employers customized programs that include everything from managing stress and clutter, to exploring the healing benefits of humor, to discussing the merits of going green, along with more traditional programs revolving around diet and exercise.

Wellness Track owner Annette Racond, a New York City-based wellness columnist and writer, believes that keeping employees healthy, happy—and green—offers considerable benefits to employers, including lower health-care costs and more productive employees, which boosts both morale and the company's bottom line.

92 Quick Tip: Gift Green

Whether it is the holiday season, or you are giving corporate or personal gifts for another reason, get into the habit of thinking green gifts. Plants, organic wines, or any number of items made from recycled materials can be both thoughtful for the individual and for the Earth. How about a fair-trade recycled corporate executive briefcase? Or a tri-fold wallet made from recycled billboard signs? Perhaps a solar panel backpack made from recycled materials? How about organic lotions or candles? There are numerous options for gifting with green products.

In addition, you can look for handmade products from local craftspeople, artisans, and manufacturers. Reduce the shipping costs by shopping close to home and buying products made in your community.

Of course, when shopping, you will also want to concern yourself with the process that produced the gifts. Think about the life cycle chain as it pertains to the gifts you would like to give. Where are the products manufactured? In what manner? By whom? How do they reach the retailer? How do they get to you? In what kind of packaging? You will also want to focus on the chain as it will continue after you have given your gifts. If they are organic, they can eventually be recycled or reused and not become part of the growing problem of waste and overflowing landfills. At first, this may be a difficult chain to put together without some research. However, in time, you will discover a process that meets your criteria. Once you find some retailers featuring quality green gifts, you can become a regular customer.

93 *Go Organic*

If you are selling food, serving food to customers or employees at an employee cafeteria, catering meetings or special events, or simply ordering in for your department, you can choose to go the organic route.

The key to organic foods is finding out how they were grown, where they come from, and what was done to them in the course of growing, preserving, packing, and shipping. The closer the foods are to being freshly grown, the more organic they are.

Section 14. Social Responsibilty and Doing Better for Your People

The first step to eating more organic foods is getting into the habit of reading labels regularly. Understand that "100 percent natural" does not necessarily mean that what you are buying is organic. Seek out organic labels that state the food contains only organically produced ingredients, free of additives, and so on. Foods that are listed as organic need to be at least 95 percent organic in their ingredients. You will also find the term *free-range* when buying meat and poultry, which typically means that the animals were allowed to run free, rather than being caged. More specifically, you'll also find the term *cage-free*.

For many people in your office, going 100 percent organic will be difficult, unless they are already used to eating in such a manner. In an effort to promote organic eating, you might start with some healthy snack foods. Put them out and don't even tell the naysayers they are organic. You can gradually build to using organic dairy products, fruits, and vegetables. You may need to spend a little more time shopping for organic meats, chicken, and fish, but once you find an organic supplier, you can become a regular customer. Of course, not all organic foods taste the same. If you are not satisfied, look for another vendor. Organic breads and pasta are fairly easy to find today. There is a steadily growing market for organic foods prompted by customer interest and requests.

Some people will choose to be vegetarians, while others will elect to continue eating meats. That's a personal choice. However, across the board, there are organic options for almost all foods today and the USDA guarantees that foods labeled organic are free of toxic pesticides, fertilizers, hormones, antibiotics, and modified organisms. If you are serving food, it behooves the modern restaurant owner to start adding some organic alternatives, as more and more people will be asking for them.

In addition to ensuring that the food was produced without chemicals or pesticides, you'll want to consider how the food was shipped. Foods shipped from distant locations utilize more packaging and require more fuel for the shipping process than those from local farmers. Supporting your local growers is both environmentally and economically sound. Again, the ideal is having the fewest number of steps between a food's origins and your plate.

Organic eating is an important step for the environment and typically a means of eating in a healthier manner. While many people will not go 100 percent organic, you will find more people opting to mix some organic choices into their menus.

To find out more about going organic, you might go to the USDA website for their agricultural marketing service at **ams.usda.gov**.

94 *Quick Tip: Create a Company Library*

In many businesses, employees read the same books, handbooks, and reports. Rather than having numerous copies, why not create a library from which people can share the same reading materials? This is a terrific means of saving paper. Of course, this does not have to pertain only to business materials. Those commuting via train or bus may have magazines, newspapers, novels, and other reading materials that can be shared. Simply set up a separate corner of the office or break room for reading materials and ask that everyone take good care of the literature and return it. This way, rather than a dozen copies of *People* magazine stashed in various desks, you'll have just a couple copies. Several small companies that have instituted shared reading with business and personal literature have found that the company library has also created a stronger bond among employees who discuss articles and novels.

Of course, this can spill over to sharing CDs or other materials. One of the characteristics of the new, environmentally focused culture is reversing the trend of individuality that has come about thanks to headphones, headsets, instant messages, and other forms of technology that have limited social interaction among people. To improve the condition of the earth and combat global warming, it is imperative that people once again communicate. Sharing, as in a library, or any other means of distributing data among several individuals in an effort to minimize materialization, is a step in the right direction.

95 *Provide Green Incentives*

O ne of the most effective ways to generate interest in any new idea is through the use of incentives. While you may not be able to afford to give bicycles to every employee, as New Belgium Brewery does, you can work within the financial and business structure you have. For example, some businesses are buying their employees lunch and giving gift cards, flex days, added personal days, or other types of incentives in return for their employees' involvement in green activities.

Of course, going green should be for the benefit of the environment, to improve personal health, and to help the planet. The idea of sustainability is still emerging; it will hopefully become part and parcel of everyone's daily life. Nonetheless, as creatures of habit, we are comfortable with the way things are, and change is often seen as more trouble than it's worth. Therefore, to battle apathy and encourage change, incentives are a good way to make inroads.

Start by looking at your sustainability plans and then at the initiatives you are promoting in your company. Determine what individual efforts need to be made to reach your goals. From there you can start putting incentives in place. If, for example, one of your objectives is to minimize an expansive parking lot around your facility by transforming some of the area to a greener landscape, you will need plans that include a strategy to reduce the need for parking spaces, a landscape plan, and a timetable for executing the plans. If employees are going to be actively involved in the process, you can determine how much time and effort is worth an incentive. Keep in mind that incentives are not to spur competition. Small incentives, in line with the efforts requested, provide added motivation, but shouldn't attract individuals who are only involved for the possibility of gaining something significant. In other words, incentives are not grand prizes.

You will also want to consider incentives for suppliers and vendors who are working in line with your efforts to be more sustainable. This will serve two purposes. First, they will be more likely to think along the same lines as your business and secondly, you can build a relationship by encouraging suppliers and vendors to work with your business on a long-term basis.

It's important, however, to emphasize not only that there are incentives for focusing on sustainability and green initiatives, but that everyone understands the bigger picture and that the incentives encourage participants' expanded understanding. In other words, you hope everyone understands, in the grand scheme of things, why they spent several days landscaping, and not just that they did a little work and got a reward.

96 Look for Transparency in Certifications and Ecolabels

It seems that every day a new certificate, seal, or label appears as the stamp of approval for environmentally sound products or services. The problem is, how do you determine who or what organization is behind the myriad possible labels, seals, and certificates of approval? While Energy Star has become a highwater mark with a transparent background that includes government backing, it is becoming harder to determine the validity of other organizations.

Section 14. Social Responsibilty and Doing Better for Your People

The new term *ecolabel* refers to a logo or stamp of approval that identifies a product or company as having met some environmentally preferable standard. The first question you may want to ask is, Who is behind the environmental ecolabel? This is where transparency becomes an issue. What can you find out about companies that use ecolabels?

First, don't immediately equate nonprofit with trustworthy. While it may be assumed that a nonprofit is more impartial than a for-profit business, simply because they should be neutral and unbiased, this is not always the case, as nonprofits may be trying to advance their own ideas or agendas. A nonprofit needs to be as transparent as any other business.

Transparency today means being able to see what makes an association or organization credible. Who is behind the screen? Is a government organization, such as the EPA, involved? Government support is typically a good sign, as is a reputation for working on environmental issues and having credible programs already in place. Look at the history of the organization and the criteria used by whoever is handing out certificates or ecolabels, to determine if they have set the bar high enough to make an impact. Also look at the process by which a business or product is reviewed or judged. Is a brief sampling used, or is a company rated on their sustainability efforts over a long period of time? Do products need to meet minimal, undemanding requirements or are there strict criteria?

There is also something to be said for an industry watchdog group that has a good reputation and past history of accomplishments. For example, the Forest Stewardship Council (**fscus.org**), was formed by loggers, foresters, environmentalists, and sociologists some 15 years ago with a mission to answer the question, What is sustainable forestry? They have worked hard to answer that question and gain the respect of the industry for their research and extensive body of work in forestry, and all of it is available for review.

Coalitions, larger ones in particular, can have a strong presence and, as a group, establish standards and criteria to be followed, such as the Sustainable Packaging Coalition (**sustainablepackaging.org**). Again, it is important that the coalition be very clear about their mission, their process of screening, and their criteria for ecolabeling. Smaller coalitions, sometimes in the growing stages, may not have (or follow) the same objectives in their efforts to simply control the industry, rather than to improve it.

Therefore, you'll want to do your research before accepting at face value that a certificate, award, seal, or logo makes a company, product, or service more sustainable or greener.

One place to look behind the labels is **ecolabelling.org**. This website provides up-to-date information on the businesses and non-profits behind over 200 ecolabels, without passing judgment.

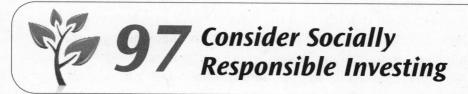

97 Consider Socially Responsible Investing

Environmentally speaking, why not put your money where your mouth is? Whether it is money invested for your business or investment choices for your employees' 401k plans, you may want to focus your attention on socially responsible investing (SRI). This is a strategy where you invest in companies that are concerned about the environment and have a social consciousness as part of their platform. An ever increasing number of mutual funds adhere to social and environmental criteria. In fact, as of early 2008, there were more than 200 SRI funds and $2.3 trillion invested in them. Investors are going this route to align their investment dollars with their business and personal beliefs. They also want to encourage more businesses to become socially responsible, and support the growth of companies already invested in making global social and environmental changes. Among the social issues incorporated into the stock selection criteria of SRI mutual funds are:

○ Workplace practices

Section 14. Social Responsibilty and Doing Better for Your People

- Human rights
- Workplace safety
- Community relations and responsibility

The environmental practices include:

- Sustainable packaging
- Type of products manufactured and/or sold
- CO_2 emissions
- Overall sustainability of the business and concern for the environment

For your purposes, before you invest, you'll want to look at the recent results in the SRI category and try to determine where the overall market is headed. Your first concern is whether or not it is a good time to invest at all, since the market today typically moves in one direction, regardless of the type of funds in which you are invested. Some financial planners and advisors will argue that perhaps you should simply invest wherever you find the greatest possible profits, make money, and then use that money to support environmental causes. However, many investors feel that you should not support companies and businesses that you do not believe are environmentally friendly or socially responsible, but rather align yourself with companies that share your beliefs.

Several of the SRI mutual funds have done very well. In fact, as of September 2007, the following funds saw 10-year average annual gains of better than 9 percent:

- Winslow Green Growth Fund
- Bridgeway Ultra Small Company Market Fund
- Parnassus Equity Income Fund
- Calvert Large Cap Growth I
- Calvert Large Cap Growth A

Another SRI fund that has a good track record is Pax World Balanced Fund, considered the forerunner of the SRI fund movement. Of course, 10-year averages only indicate past performance and not what a fund will do in the future. On a positive note, 10 years with positive gains show survival in a bear market through the first half of the decade. Note on selecting mutual funds: Keep in mind, when looking at mutual funds, that average annual return is not as true an indicator of success as compounded annual return. The reason is that if you saw a return of 14 percent over five years, you will have doubled your investment because the investment is compounding annually. Therefore, rather than 14 percent x 5 or a 70 percent return, you would make a 100 percent return on your initial invest- ment. Average annual returns will show you 100 percent divided by 5, or a 20 percent average annual return, which isn't really the case, but looks better for those selling investment products.

Since not all SRI funds are the same, you'll want to look at the top holdings to see if they meet your criteria for environmental and socially responsible investing. One person may not flinch because a company invests in a business that makes beer, provided the business is green in their process, such as the New Belgium Brewing Company (whose stock is not on the market yet but uses sustainable business practices). Someone else will rule out any businesses that make alcohol. The point is, there are criteria set forth by fund managers and criteria set forth by you as the investor. You also may find that you have no problem with the products produced by a company, but through research, learn that they are major polluters or use sweatshop labor.

Of course, you do not only have to invest in mutual funds. You can buy individual stocks in companies that you believe meet your social and environmental criteria. You can also invest in real estate that is being used for environmentally sound practices. The key is to follow your belief system with your investments, whatever they are.

Along with investing your own company or personal funds, you can spread the SRI concept by making such investment options available to your employees, which may be through their 401k plans or through socially responsible investment seminars or handouts.

You can also make a statement as an investor by becoming a shareholder and attending shareholder meetings where you discuss and even question the sustainability of a company. More and more investors are speaking up and voicing concerns to corporate man- agement by becoming shareholders.

For more on becoming a socially and environmentally responsible investor, go to **socialfunds.com**.

98 Buy Carbon Offsets

"Carbon neutral" has become the catchphrase of the new green generation, so much so that it was the new word of the year in the 2006 New Oxford American Dictionary. It means to neutralize the amount of carbon you produce, which is your carbon footprint. If you can offset your entire carbon footprint, you are carbon neutral.

The first way to offset your carbon footprint, or carbon expenditure, is to do whatever you can to reduce carbon emissions. Many of the suggestions in this book and from numerous websites, magazine articles, and media releases provide ways to save energy and reduce carbon output. However, it is almost impossible for most businesses to become carbon neutral or have a zero carbon footprint through their own actions and efforts. Even businesses with the best environmental intentions will end up using some amount of fossil fuel or traditional energy resources in some aspect of their daily operations.

That is where carbon offsets *should* come in. We'll explain the *should* later.

Carbon offsets are a very basic concept. You calculate the carbon footprint of your business and buy carbon offsets to reduce an equal amount of carbon elsewhere, which theoretically counterbalances the carbon emissions from your energy-using activities. Since the average American is responsible for 10 tons of CO_2 emissions annually through his or her personal activities, it can be assumed that most small businesses will be responsible for at least that amount.

Buying carbon offsets means that you are putting money toward any of the thousands of carbon-reducing projects, such as those involved with renewable energy, energy efficiency, or reforestation.

Section 14. Social Responsibilty and Doing Better for Your People

The reason we say *should* is because buying carbon offsets, for many businesses, is akin to writing a check rather than getting their hands dirty. It bespeaks less than a wholehearted commitment. Carbon offsets should follow your own efforts to be more energy-efficient and environmentally sensitive in your business practices. They should not be used as an easy means to ease your corporate conscience. Large corporations that specialize in pollution and add to our landfills are not necessarily making a fair exchange by purchasing carbon offsets for projects that, in many instances, will take place in the future. Therefore, carbon offsets should follow your own green activities. What you cannot accomplish on your own can be offset by the purchasing of carbon offsets.

One carbon offset represents the reduction of one metric ton of carbon dioxide, or its equivalent in other greenhouse gases, such as methane. Carbon offsets vary in price, but in the United States they are typically between $5 and $18 each. Therefore, if your business vehicle produces three tons of CO_2 per year, you could offset that for less than $40. Of course, you could buy a hybrid car, cut the number to 1.5 tons, and offset the rest.

Carbon offsets are easy to purchase. However, you may want to know a little more about how your money is being spent. Here are a few places to visit online to get an idea of how they use the funding when buying their carbon offsets:

- Atmosclear at **atmosclear.org**
- The Carbonfund at **Carbonfund.org**
- e-Blue Horizons at **e-bluehorizons.net**
- Eco2Pass at **eco2pass.com**
- Greenoffice at **thegreenoffice.com**
- Native Energy at **nativeenergy.com**
- Natsource at **natsource.com**

These are just a few of the many places where you can purchase carbon offsets. Based on more than $91 million in voluntary offsets sold in 2006 (some countries have a cap over which you have to buy offsets), it is estimated that the number topped $100 million in 2007; it is still climbing in 2008.

Section 14. Social Responsibilty and Doing Better for Your People

If you look at carbon offsetting on **ecobusinesslinks.com**, you'll find information and prices for various carbon offsetting sellers, plus the type of offsets sold and the type of projects your money is going to support. Another website, called Cleanair-coolplanet (**cleanair-coolplanet.org**) is another place where you can learn about the wide range of carbon offsets.

While carbon offsets are a plausible and well intended means of financing global environmental change, critics have two problems with the overall concept.

First, there is no centrally recognized regulation at present, meaning you do not necessarily know what you are buying. There are certificates from the Chicago Climate Exchange, Environmental Resources Exchange, and other worthwhile organizations, but because the field is so new, there is little hard evidence of the success of the programs being supported. In other words, the trees have not yet grown in many cases. Other concerns are for the upkeep and maintenance of such projects after their initial activities. For example, are the trees your offset dollars planted being cut down or destroyed? While the dollars raised by offsets are earmarked for many good projects (not just involving trees) at present, there is still some degree of uncertainty about the potential success of some of the projects.

The second issue often raised is whether or not you are paying someone to do work that was going to be done anyway, in which case you are not really reducing your carbon footprint. "Is there additionality?" That's the question as posed by Anne Bedarf, project manager at **GreenBlue.org**, a Virginia-based nonprofit institute that focuses on the expertise of professional communities to create practical solutions, resources, and opportunities for implementing sustainability.

Yes, carbon offsets may indeed be the next great thing in lowering the carbon emissions for our planet. No, they are not a pass to do whatever you choose and then simply offset your actions. The hope is that the majority of the funds used for carbon offsets are properly utilized and that the organizations selling these offsets can help us continue directing environmental endeavors in the right direction.

Some Final Suggestions

99 Rate Your Own Corporate Citizenship

What do the following 10 companies have in common?

1. Green Mountain Coffee Roasters, Inc.
2. Advanced Micro Devices, Inc.
3. Nike, Inc.
4. Motorola, Inc.
5. Intel Corporation
6. International Business Machines Corporation
7. Agilent Technologies, Inc.
8. Timberland Company
9. Starbucks Corporation
10. General Mills, Inc.

They comprise *Business Ethics Magazine's* list of the top 10 corporate citizens of 2007, as compiled by KLD Research & Analytics, Inc. For a list of the Top 100, go to **kld.com/research/socrates/ businessethics100/2007**. Other companies, such as Whole Foods Market, Wal-Mart, and Costco, to name a few, are also among the major players in the environmental movement and good corporate citizens.

While it may take a small to midsize business a little longer to become recognized in such a significant manner, the examples set by these companies are noteworthy. Researching their ESG (environmental, social and governance) is certainly worth exploring.

What can you do? Utilize some of the categories provided as criteria for corporate citizenship to rate where you stand. These include shareholders, community, diversity, employees, environment, human rights, and product. You can also add customer relations. Evaluate where you stand in each area.

For example:

○ Are you transparent with your shareholders and do you incorporate their ideas and concerns into your strategies?

- Are you involved in the community?
- Do you sponsor community activities and take part in community efforts and projects?
- Do you embrace diversity in the workplace?
- Do you treat your employees with the dignity and respect they deserve?
- Do you offer health benefits and other types of assistance?
- Do you offer incentives or rewards?
- Are you working toward sustainability?
- Have you instituted environmental goals, plans, and initiatives in all areas of your business?
- Do you support, defend, and work to improve the rights of workers here and abroad?
- Are your products in step with your corporate citizenship and do they represent your company's beliefs?

You do not have to make any top 10 or top 100 list to justify that your business is indeed making a positive impact on this planet. In recent years, it has become clear that social and environmental responsibility are two components to what has emerged as a three-tiered business model, or a triple bottom line.

One, a socially-responsible business embraces people, which translates to happy, healthy employees, which tends to increase your customer base. Two, an environmentally-consciuous business can save money in various areas while helping the planet and attracting more business through its eco-awareness. Three, a financially-successful business has found a successful means of attracting and keeping their customers by providing excellent products and/or services at good prices.

See if all three tiers in your business are where you would like them to be. If not, now is the time to start becoming a better corporate citizen by following the example set by the above-mentioned companies.

100 *Teach Future Generations*

Are there kid-friendly versions of your products? Do you have a children's menu? Does your waiting room have kid-friendly games? Does your website have a children's section?

While parents are the decision makers, many businesses today are looking to attract a young audience as well. As we explore and embrace new forms of environmental activities and policies, it is important that the next generation learn what sustainability is all about. After all, if young children start out with a greater understanding of how to treat Mother Earth with respect, they will not foster the same bad habits that have put us in this quandary.

You can take time to attract young customers while also educating them about the environment and what it means to be an environmentally-concerned citizen. This can be done in one of several ways:

- **Speaking at schools:** Whether it is part of an assembly or in individual classrooms (which is more effective), you can discuss what your business is doing to benefit the environment. Not only is this a valuable lesson for children, but you can be sure they will tell their parents that they want to shop at your store or on your website.

- **Sponsor an outdoor activity:** Think of something that kids enjoy, whether it is a sporting activity, a carnival, or a picnic and do it. Make it a green event; from healthy, organic foods to kid-friendly activities, you can make an impact.

- **Offer tours of your facility:** This will depend on the nature of the business. However, if you put the right spin on it, you can make almost anything interesting to young children—just remember who your audience is.

- **Write it:** If you are in any type of publishing business—books, magazines or producing CDs—you can write about ways to benefit the environment. The same holds true for the literature that comes with toys and games. Make sure it is recyclable and that young readers understand what that means.

○ **Internships:** For high-schoolers, you might inquire about having an intern program in which students can work in your company and see firsthand what it is to be part of a green business.

The goal is to teach sustainability and ways to make greener products or conduct a greener business, so the next generation can start out several steps ahead of where we are today, with eco-friendly practices being second nature to them.

101 *Don't Stop*

One of the problems with starting a diet, making a New Year's resolution, or promising that you will make a change in lifestyle, is that after a few days, weeks, or perhaps months, most of us tend to slide back to our old habits. Many green initiatives and plans to be 'more environmentally conscious' have also fallen by the wayside simply because people lost sight of the long-term significance of maintaining such policies.

For this reason, it is vital that you set up benchmarks and ongoing meetings to review where you are on your quest to become *and remain* a sustainable business. Schedule quarterly sustainability reports and have initiatives that are set up well in advance with markers along the way. If you find yourself slipping because of the many responsibilities that come with being an entrepreneur, then delegate the job to someone, or hire a sustainability manager or director.

It is also important to have staff members who keep the ball rolling by finding internet stories of green activities that other businesses are doing, as well as stories pointing out the ongoing problems.

Section 15. Some Final Suggestions

This is also a good reason for incentives, which can help to keep everyone looking toward the future and thinking green on an ongoing basis. Place incentives six months or one year down the road. Also, make sure your efforts are visible, with desk-side recycling bins and, if necessary, signs reminding people to recycle or to use only green cleaning products.

It's easy to lose sight of environmental goals because you are not necessarily seeing the results of your efforts. Sending an e-mail around letting people know how much you have saved on your energy bill, or how many pounds of materials your business has recycled in the past month or year, is one way to show everyone and thank them for their efforts. However, you will not likely see the results of the big picture, such as the lower pollution levels in your community. With that in mind, outdoor cleanups are a good eye-opener, and working on green acreage puts the picture in a little more perspective.

No, it's not easy to stay on that diet or keep that New Year's resolution for the entire year. However, it is possible if your entire business buys into the need for sustainability and greener business practices. Do whatever you need to do to keep it going.

Putting It All Together

Now that you have read through the 101 ways you can make your business greener, you should have a better understanding of what green is all about. Utilizing some of these suggestions along with your own industry-specific ideas will make you a more sustainable business and reduce your carbon imprint. How will this effort to improve your environmental stance make you more profitable?

Profits are based on a variety of factors, including the costs it takes to run your business, from ordering products to spreading the word through advertising and promotion to having all of the necessary equipment in working order. Introducing many of the environmentally-friendly suggestions in this book will bring down your expenses, not necessarily immediately, but in time. Lower expenses allow you to enjoy a greater profit margin on products and/or services as well as price yourself competitively within your field. As your overhead comes down, thanks to lower electric bills (by using renewable energy sources, such as wind turbine power), you can charge lower prices to draw customers away from your competitors who need to charge more to pay their energy bills.

Another means of generating more profit by going green is simply appealing to the quickly growing environmentally conscious audience. If you are sustainable, word will spread because you are part of the solution and not the problem, and consumers want to be on the right side of the eco-crisis. The number of articles about green businesses is increasing on a daily basis. No longer are such articles reserved for environmental and niche magazines. Today you will find *The New York Times*, *The Wall Street Journal*, and the most popular magazines all printing articles about green businesses and eco-friendly companies. Use public relations to help spread the word about what you are up to. This can also serve to build community awareness.

Profits will also come by way of innovation. New bamboo flooring, bamboo clothing, an original formula for an organic face cream, body lotion, or shampoo, the latest in hybrid automobile technology, or a software program that helps track your energy and fuel usage,

Section 16. Putting It All Together

are all examples of new inventions that have drawn attention in a market looking for green solutions. Focus on finding a more environmentally friendly way to solve a common concern, and you can enjoy a windfall of profits along with the satisfaction of making a positive impact on the planet.

And finally, being socially responsible pays off in less tangible, but also profitable, ways. By providing your employees with some of the benefits mentioned within the 101 suggestions, whether it is telecommuting, flex days, or incentives for going green, and by offering a health plan, you are more likely to see less absenteeism, less turnover, and higher morale. Introducing green projects and getting your crew involved in more than just the business aspect of their jobs, but also touching on the broader picture, such as the community and environmental issues, boosts the team atmosphere and instills a sense of loyalty to your business. And remember: A happy team can produce more and generate greater profits than a staff of employees who have one foot out the door, ready to seek other employment opportunities. It also costs far less money to attract and keep highly skilled top people than it does to have to train new people on a regular basis.

Environmental, social, and financial—the three sides to the triangle are now complete. These are the areas you will need to focus on in order to make a major dent in today's environmentally-conscious, always competitive business world.

Go back, look at the 101 suggestions and decide which 5, 10, or 20 you can implement in time and with the dedication of your team. Share the book, share the ideas, and invite new suggestions. As I wrote number 101, I realized there were plenty more, so please feel free to add ideas and send me your thoughts in the event we have an addendum on the next printing.

Stay green,
Rich Mintzer
rsmz@optonline.net

APPENDIX A

Glossary

Biodegradable The ability of a substance to be broken down physically and/or chemically by microorganisms. Natural and organic products are typically biodegradable, while many man-made plastics or materials, such as polyester, generally are not.

Biofuel A source of fuel made from renewable or recyclable natural energy sources. This includes biodiesel fuels typically made from vegetable oils.

Carbon footprint A measure of the amount of carbon dioxide or CO_2 emitted by a business or individual as part of their daily operations.

Carbon neutral Also known as carbon zero, this is where you are either emitting no carbon dioxide into the atmosphere or balancing the amount of carbon dioxide emitted in another manner.

Carbon offsets A means of achieving carbon neutrality by paying for ecological and environmentally beneficial projects in other parts of the country or the world, to balance the amount of carbon dioxide your business is emitting into the atmosphere. (Green tags for travel are a similar concept.)

Compostable Naturally grown or harvested materials (from plants or animal tissues) that will decompose in the environment.

Composting A process of utilizing organic materials (typically garbage and scraps) to create fertilizer for soil and plants.

Cradle to cradle The making of products that can be beneficial to the environment from their initial creation through their use and even after their initial use as waste.

Eco-friendly (also environmentally friendly) Both terms refer to ways and means of operating a business or using materials and products that are not harmful to the planet by way of greenhouse gas, CO_2 emissions, being non-biodegradable, or being toxic.

Eco-labels (or Ecolabels) The labeling of products whose ingredients and/or means of generating the product are eco-friendly (e.g., organically grown). Also refers to certifications or labeling by an organization, association, or other group.

Appendix A. Glossary

Electronic waste Also known as e-waste; comprised of computers and other high-tech machines that are no longer being used and often end up in landfills, rather than being recycled.

Energy Star A joint program of the U.S. Environmental Protection Agency and the U.S. Department of Energy that provides designation of products that are identified as energy-efficient.

Environmentally Preferable Purchasing (EPP) Buying products that have a minimal or reduced level of negative impact on the environment rather than buying products that leave a negative mark on the environment.

Flexible-fuel vehicles (FFV) Vehicles that typically have separate gas tanks for different types of fuels.

Global warming The name given to the warming of the earth's atmosphere because greenhouses gases are preventing the heat from escaping. (See greenhouse effect)

Green building The practice of building structures utilizing environmentally friendly materials and designed to operate in an ecological manner that uses natural resources and leaves a minimal carbon footprint.

Greenhouse effect The effect caused by the earth's heat being held in place by gasses in the earth's atmosphere such as carbon dioxide (CO_2), methane (CH_4), and nitrous oxide (N_2O), otherwise known as greenhouse gases. The result is global warming. This is similar to the manner in which a greenhouse maintains heat.

Greenwashing The practice of misleading the public by creating a pro-environmental image while not actually following environmental and/or ecological practices.

Hazardous waste Unused or discarded materials of any kind that emit toxins or other substances into the air or water that can be dangerous to humans, wildlife, or plants.

Hybrid car An automobile that uses both a combustion (fossil-fuel-burning) engine and an electric motor powered by batteries.

Landfill A means of final disposal of solid waste on land. The refuse/waste is compacted and spread out in layers of soil, and remains intact for years.

LEED-certified A designation by the United States Green Building Council's Leadership in Energy and Environmental Design (LEED) indicating that either a building, architect, or the material used in the building process meets sustainable green building and development standards.

Life cycle The course of a product from the growth of its initial materials to the end of the product's components when recycled or disposed of as waste.

Organic Naturally grown materials without the use of fossil fuels or any type of chemicals.

Passive solar heating and cooling A means of using natural methods to heat or cool a building by utilizing or blocking sunlight at various times of day and storing heat or cool air in the facility.

Pollution The process in which substances that are toxic to humans, animals, or plants are emitted into the air, water, or soil.

Post-consumer recycled content Material used by consumers and then recycled into another product.

Postmanufacturer recycled content Content made from the waste generated in the manufacturing of another product.

Recyclable The broad term used to indicate that the materials used in a product can be reused in another product. There are numerous methods in which various materials, such as plastics, are melted down in the recycling process. Recycling is also often used to refer to the reuse of a product by one person after it has been used by another, thus maintaining the usefulness of the item.

Reuse Utilizing a product for another purpose after its initial intended purpose to maintain the life and usefulness of the product. Unlike recycling, the item is typically not altered.

Appendix A. Glossary

Socially responsible A manner of describing a business or an organization that is proactive in terms of doing positive things for their employees, their community, and society at large.

Socially responsible investing (SRI) Investing in businesses, mutual funds, or other investment vehicles that use social and environmental criteria to mirror your own beliefs.

Sustainability The practice of maintaining a life cycle that goes from nature back to nature, using as little man-made energy as possible.

Transparency In business today, this term refers to making your goals, motives, and means of operations clear and open to being observed or reviewed by the public.

U-factor The measure of heat that penetrates through a glass window

Vermicomposting Composting using worms (see composting)

Volatile organic compounds (VOC) Organic compounds that evaporate readily into the air. These are typically not good for clean air quality; they include substances such as benzene, methylene chloride, and methyl chloroform.

Waste management The process of finding and utilizing ways of limiting waste and/or preventing waste from ending up in landfills.

Waste prevention The act of making decisions that will minimize the generation of any type of waste.

Xeriscaping The practice of landscaping with slow-growing, drought-tolerant plants.

Resources

Below is an alphabetical list of online environmental resources, including government agencies, alliances, nonprofit associations, organizations, and companies that are leaders in the environmental effort. Naturally, these are just some of the many environmentally active organizations and companies.

20/20 Vision.org, **2020vision.org**

Air & Waste Management Association, **awma.org**

Alliance for America, **allianceforamerica.org**

Alliance to Save Energy, **ase.org**

American Council for an Energy Efficient Economy, **aceee.org**

American Forest & Paper Association, **afandpa.org**

American Forests, **americanforests.org**

American Water Resources Association, **awra.org**

American Water Works Association, **awwa.org**

American Wind Energy Association, **awea.org**

Better World Club, **Betterworldclub.com**

Business & Institutional Furniture Manufacturer's Association:
   bifma.org

Carbon Fund, **carbonfund.org**

Carpet America Recovery Effort (CARE), **carpetrecovery.org**

Center for Biological Diversity, **biologicaldiversity.org**

Center for Small Business & the Environment,
   geocities.com/aboutcsbe

CleanAir-CoolPlanet, **cleanair-coolplanet.org**

Clean Air Trust, **cleanairtrust.org**

Clean Water Fund, **cleanwaterfund.org**

Collective Good International, **collectivegood.com**

Compostsites Fabricators Association, **acmanet.org**

Computer Recycling, **computerrecyclingdirectory.com**

Conservation International, **conservation.org**

Conservatree, **conservatree.com**

Appendix B. Resources

Container Recycling Institute, **container-recycling.org**

Co-op America, **coopamerica.org**

Cool Roof Rating Council, **coolroofs.org**

Database of State Incentives for Renewables and Efficiency,
dsireusa.org

Defenders of Wildlife, **defenders.org**

Earth 911, **earth911.org**

Earth Animal, **earthanimal.com**

Earth Force, **earthforce.org**

Earth Share, **earthshare.org**

Earthwatch, **earthwatch.org**

EcoMall, **ecomall.com**

Eco-Office, **eco-office.com**

Electronics Recycling Infrastructure Clearinghouse,
ecyclingresource.org

Energy Savers, **energysavers.gov**

Energy Star, **energystar.com**

Envirolink Network, **envirolink.org**

Environmental Protection Agency, (EPA), **epa.gov**

Environmental Support Center, **envsc.org**

Environmental Technology Council, **etc.org**

Flexcar, **flexcar.com**

Forest Stewardship Council, **fsc.org**

Green Biz Leaders, **greenbizleaders.com**

Green Building Exchange, **greenbuildingexchange.com**

Green Business Alliance, **greenbusinessalliance.com**

Green Globe, **ec3global.com**

Green Office, **thegreenoffice.com**

Green Pages Co-op, **greenpages.org**

Green Seal, **greenseal.org**

GreenBiz, **greenbiz.com**

GreenBlue, **greenblue.org**

Greenguard, **greenguard.org**

Insulation Contractors Association of America, **insulate.org**

International Network for Environmental Management, **inem.org**

National Brownfield Association, **brownfieldassociation.org**

National Council for Air & Stream Improvement, Inc., **ncasi.org**

National Ethanol Vehicle Coalition, **e85fuel.com**

National Fenestration Ratings Council, **nfrc.org**

National Insulation Association, **insulation.org**

National Recycling Coalition, **nrc-recycle.org**

National Solid Waste Management Association, **nswma.org**

National Wildlife Federation, **nwf.org**

Natural Environmental Directory, **environmentaldirectory.net**

Natural Resources Defense Council, **nrdc.org**

Nature Conservancy, **nature.org**

One Percent for the Planet, **onepercentfortheplanet.org**

Planet Green, **planetgreen.com**

RideSpring, **ridespring.com**

SaveOurEnvironment, **saveourenvironment.org,**

Seventh Generation, **seventhgeneration.com**

Sierra Club, **sierraclub.org**

Social Investment Forum, **socialinvest.org**

Society for Ecological Restoration, **ser.org**

Society of the Plastics Industry, **socplas.org**

Sonoco Sustainability Solutions, **sonoco.com**

Sustainable Forestry Initiative (SFI), **aboutsfi.org**

Sustainable Packaging Coalition, **sustainablepackaging.org**

The Daily Green, **thedailygreen.com**

The International Ecotourism Society (TIES), **ecotourism.org**

Treehugger, **treehugger.com**

Trees for Travel, **treesfortravel.info**

Appendix B. Resources

Union of Concerned Scientists, **ucsusa.org**

United States Department of Energy, Office of Energy Efficiency and Renewable Energy, **http://eere.energy.gov**

United States Green Building Council (USGBC) (developers of the LEED ratings system), **usgbc.org**

Word of Mouth Marketing Association, **womma.org**

ZeroFootprint.com, **zerofootprint.com**

Zipcar, **zipcar.com**

Here are 10 of the many smaller businesses out there that have embraced green and proved helpful in this book:

ClifBar, **clifbar.com**

Curtis Packaging, **curtispackaging.com**

Denim Therapy, **denimtherapy.com**

Eco Timber, **ecotimber.com**

Green Diamond Tires Company, **greendiamondtire.com**

Kelly LaPlante Organic Design, **organicinteriordesign.com**

New Belgium Brewery, **newbelgium.com**

Newman Building Designs, **newmanbuildingdesigns.com**

Pangea Organics, **pangeaorganics.com**

Solar Wind Works, **solarwindworks.com**

Index

A

Accountability of telecommuters, 148–149

Active chilled beams, 49

Adjustable shades, 45–46

Advanced Micro Devices, 145

Air, shipping, 125

Air conditioners, covering, 36–37. *See also* Cooling systems

Air-Conditioning and Refrigeration Institute, 30

Air filtration, indoor plants for, 65–66

Air flow. *See* Ventilation

Air leakage, 35, 36

Air quality, 116–117, 187. *See also* Ventilation

Aluminum bottles, 82

Aluminum cans, 17

American Council for an Energy-Efficient Economy, 27

American Marketing Association, 172

Answering machines, 102–103

Anti-letter campaigns, 113–114

Apple computers, 95

Appliances, energy efficient, 26–27

Architects, 186, 187

Aveda, 79

Average annual returns, 219

Average annual wind speed, 52–53

AXA Financial, 209

B

Bags, reusable, 85–87, 113

Bamboo
fabrics made from, 133, 168
flooring, 54–55
furniture, 13, 41

Bank of America Tower, 184

Banner Bank Building, 184

Basketball shoes, 113

Bathrooms, 42

Batteries, rechargeable, 101–102

Battery banks, 51

Beams, chilled, 49

Beer bottles, 78, 82

Beer making, 112, 133

Better World Club, 143–144

Bicycles
commuting via, 145–146
promoting ridership, 199
renting while traveling, 151
small shipments via, 129

Biodegradable packing peanuts, 83

Biodegradable party supplies, 108

Bio-plastics, 134–135

Bottled water, 61, 79

Bottleless water coolers, 62

Bottles, 78, 82

Breweries, 112, 133

Brit's Pub, 48

Brownfields, 188–190

Bubble wrap, 15, 83

Buildings. *See also* Offices
brownfield, 188–190

Index

Buildings (*continued*)
   choosing greener, 183–186
   downsizing, 192–193
   expanding, 186–188
   green space around, 191–192
   offering tours, 202, 227
Business cards, 73
Business practices, examining, 4
Business travel, 150–153

C

Carbon calculators, 11
Carbon footprints, 10–11
Carbon neutrality, 10, 220
Carbon offsets, 24, 220–222
Carpet America Recovery Effort,
   165–166
Carpeting
   alternatives to, 54–55
   eco-friendly types, 12
   recycling, 165–166
Carpooling, 145, 146
Cars. *See* Vehicles
Cartridge recycling, 96
Caulk, 34
Cell phones, 99–101
Certification
   cleaning products, 115
   forest products, 13, 40–41
   validity of, 215–217
Chairs, 13
Chemicals
   foods free of, 212
   used in producing fibers, 167, 168
   in water, 62, 63
Chicago City Hall, 48
Children, teaching sustainability,
   227–228
Chilled beams, 49
Chlorine-free paper, 71
Cisterns, 64

Clean Air and Water Acts, 206
Clean Air Communities, 48
Clean diesels, 140
Cleaning products, 25, 114–116
Clif Bar, 197, 199, 204
Climate controls. *See* HVAC systems; Ventilation
Clinton Presidential Library, 184
Clorox cleaners, 132
Clothing
   eco-friendly, 133, 167–168
   recycling, 166
Cloth towels, 42
Coalitions, 216–217
Coca-Cola, 79
Coffee cups, 80, 157–158
Coffee farmers, 202
Coffee filters, 157
Coffeemakers, 157
Colangelo, Robert, 190
Coltan, 100
Communications
   coordinating for green activities,
      203–204
   green marketing, 171–174
   from sustainability directors,
      164–165
   for telecommuters, 148
   word-of-mouth, 173, 174–176
Community service, employee
   time for, 197–198
Community sustainability efforts,
   173, 203–204
Commuting, 145–150
Compact fluorescent light bulbs,
   28–29
Company libraries, 213–214
Company-wide surveys, 160
Company-wide volunteer programs, 197–198
Competition, 6

Composting, 109–111
Compounded annual return, 219
Computers
    eco-friendly, 92–95
    in-store kiosks, 193
    recycling and reusing, 96–97, 166
    using efficiently, 91–92
Conde Nast Building, 184
Conferences on sustainability, 173, 201
Consortium for Energy Efficiency, 30
Construction. *See* Buildings
Consultants, 7, 8
Consumer benefits, marketing, 173–174
Consumer recycling programs, 165–167
Contaminants in water, 62, 63
Contaminated sites, 188–190
Cooling systems
    examining during energy audits, 8
    in green buildings, 184
    upgrading and maintaining, 30–32
Cool Roof Rating Council, 47
Co-op offices, 38–39
Core values, 162
Cork flooring, 55
Corn-based labels, 81
Corporate citizenship ratings, 225–226
Cotton, 167, 168
Covers for vents and air conditioners, 36–37
CPU fans, 94
Cruise industry, 125–126
Cups, reusable, 113
Curt Chrome, 80
Curtis Packaging, 80

Cushion Cubes, 84
Customer surveys, 176–178
Cycle counting, 130

D
Dell computers, 95
Dematerializing, 166–167
Denim Therapy, 166
Design
    of offices, 11–13, 40–41
    of packaging, 79–81
Detergents, 25
Diesel engines, 140
Direct deposit, 99
Direct Marketing Association, 118
Directors of sustainability, 163–165
Distribution centers, 129
DocuSign, 98
Donations, 200
Doors, 8, 34–36
Downsizing, 192–193
Drain cleaning, 42
Dress codes, 167
Drinking water filtration, 61–63
Ducts, insulating, 31, 32–33

E
E85 fuel, 139
Earth-First® PLA label materials, 81
Ecolabelling.org, 217
Ecolabels, 216–217
Ecological Mail Coalition, 118
Ecotainers, 80
EcoTimber, 54–55
Eco-Toolbox, 80
Ecotourism, 144
E-cycling programs, 96–97
Electric service, 50–54
Electronic devices. *See also* Computers
    energy use modes, 26–27, 91

Index

Electronic devices (*continued*)
 recycling, 96–101
Employees
 green, 207–208
 impact of sustainability on
  morale, 234
 promoting wellness of, 209–210
 volunteer hours for, 197–198
Empty vehicles, avoiding, 125–126
Energy audits, 7–9
Energy Star Interactive Manage-
 ment Program, 9
Energy Star program
 appliance ratings, 26
 auditing software, 9
 battery charger ratings, 101
 computer ratings, 93
 HVAC system ratings, 30
Enterprise asset management, 131
Envelopes, reusable, 25
Enviromedia, 172
Environmental groups, supporting,
 198–201
Environmentally Preferable
 Purchasing, 14
EPA newsletter, 204
Equipment for telecommuters, 149
e-signatures, 98
Estee Lauder, 80
Ethanol, 139
Ethical Travel Guide, 151
Excelsior, 84
Excess inventory, 129–131
Excess printing, 72
Expanding buildings, 186–188
EZ Save software, 94

F
Fabricated soft foam, 83–84
Fabrics
 eco-friendly, 167–168
 recycled, 13, 166

Facilities. *See* Buildings; Offices
Facility tours, 202, 227
Fans, 32
Faucet leaks, 60
Featherfiber, 112
Filters
 air, 116–117
 indoor plants as, 65–66
 water, 61–63
First steps, 4
Flexcar, 146
Flexible-fuel vehicles, 139
Flooring, 54–55
Foam packing, 83–84
Foil alternatives, 80
Ford Escape hybrid, 141
Ford Motor Company, 48
Forest Stewardship Council, 13,
 41, 216
Fossil fuels, 10. *See also* Petroleum
Free-range meats, 212
Fresh air. *See* Ventilation
Fuel-efficient vehicles, 139–141
Fujitsu computers, 95
Furniture, 12, 13, 40–41

G
Garbage, composting, 109–111
Gardens, rooftop, 47–48, 191
Gifts, 210–211
GO GREEN! newsletter, 204
Gore, Al, 3
Governments
 lending credibility to organiza-
  tions, 216
 lobbying, 205–207
 sustainability incentives, 50, 150
Grade numbers, 17–18
Graphics cards, 92, 95
GreenBlue.org, 222
Green building goals, 187. *See
 also* Buildings

Green businesses, rationale for, 3–4
Green Cell foam, 84
Green Diamond Tires Company, 143
Green mapping, 203
Green marketing, 171–174
Green Mountain Coffee Roasters, 80
Green Seal standards, 14, 115
Green spaces, 191–192
Green tags, 152–153
Green teams, 159–161
GreenTravelPartners.com, 144
Greenwashing, 124, 171, 174
Green Works cleaners, 132
Grocery bags, 85–87

H
Health and wellness, 209–210
Heating systems
    examining during energy audits, 8
    in green buildings, 184
    passive solar, 45–47
    upgrading and maintaining, 30–32
Heat-shrink labels, 82
Hemp, 168
HEPA filters, 116
Herman Miller, 13
High-density polyethylene, 18
High-efficiency power supplies, 27
Holiday party waste, 108–109
Homebased businesses, 38–41
Honda Civic hybrid, 141
HP Compaq computers, 95
Humus, 111
HVAC systems
    in green buildings, 183–184
    passive solar, 45–47

upgrading and maintaining, 30–32
Hybrid vehicles, 140, 141

I
Idling by computers, 93–94
IKEA, 166
Incentives
    with customer surveys, 176
    effective use of, 214–215
    to encourage commitment, 229
    for finding eco-friendly supplies, 25
    for green team participants, 160
    for recycling, 17
    for renewable energy use, 50
    for saving vehicle fuel, 145–146, 150
    for sustainable packaging, 79, 86
An Inconvenient Truth, 3
Indoor air, 116–117
Industry watchdog groups, 216
Infor EAM software, 131
Inks, 72
Innovation, profits and, 233–234
Insecticides, 167
Insulation, 31, 32–34
Insulation Contractors Association of America, 33
InterFace carpet tiles, 12
Internal shipping, 128–129
The International Ecotourism Society, 144
International Paper, 80
Internships, 228
In-transit meetings, 147
Inventories, 129–131, 193
Investments, 217–220
Ionizing purifiers, 116–117
iPods, 175

Index

J

Jessup Manufacturing Company, 73
Junk mail, 118–119

K

King, Ron, 32
Kiosks, 193
Knoll, 13
Kraft Foods, 80

L

Labels, 81–82
Land use goals, 187. *See also* Locations
Laptop computers, 92
Leadership in Energy and Environmental Design, 183, 188
Lead-free circuitry, 94
Leaking faucets, 60
LED bulbs, 28, 29
LED Exit signs, 73
Legislation, lobbying for, 205–207
Leventro computers, 95
Lexus RX 400 hybrid, 141
Libraries, 167, 213–214
Light bulbs, 28–29
Lighting
    energy-efficient types, 25, 28–29
    in green buildings, 184
    for meetings, 158
Light sensors, 29
Lithium-ion, 102
Litter, 113–114
Lobbying, 205–207
Locally made gifts, 211
Local suppliers, finding, 127–128
Locations
    brownfield, 188–190
    downsizing, 192–193
    expanding, 186–188
    greener buildings, 183–186
    green space around, 191–192
Low-density polyethylene, 18
Low-flow bathroom fixtures, 42

M

MacBook Air, 95
MacBook Paper, 95
Magazines, 6
Magnetic register sheets, 37
Maintaining HVAC systems, 31
Manufacturing greener products, 131–133
Marketing, 171–176
Media blitzes, 178–179
Meetings
    greener practices, 158–159
    of green teams, 160–161
    in-transit, 147
Modeling sustainability, 201–202
Modes of use (electronics), 27, 91
Music Today, 191
Music trade magazines, 6
Mutual funds, 217–219

N

Nash, Steve, 113
National Brownfield Association, 190
National Fenestration Ratings Council, 35
National Insulation Association, 34
Natural lighting, 158, 184
Nau Inc., 125, 193
Net metering, 51
New Belgium Brewery, 112, 191, 200, 201
New construction, 189
Newsletters, 204–205
News releases, 173
Nickel-metal hydride batteries, 102
Nike, 113

Noise pollution, 178–179
Nonprofit organizations, 198–201, 215–217
North Pacific Gyre, 114
Note paper, 70

O

Oberon, 112
Office Max, 166
Offices. *See also* Buildings
    downsizing, 192–193
    eco-friendly design, 11–13, 40–41
    eco-friendly supplies, 23–26
    greener buildings, 183–186
    lighting systems, 28–29
    recycling programs, 16–17
    sharing, 38–39, 193
    sharing resources in, 37–38, 193
Office supplies. *See* Supplies
Older buildings, 185–186
1% for the Planet, 200
Onysko, Joshua, 10
Organic cotton, 168
Organic foods, 109, 211–213
Outdoor signs, 73–74
Overbuying, 15
Overruns, printing, 72
Ozone generators, 117

P

Packaging
    coalitions for sustainability in, 217
    labels, 81–82
    minimizing and redesigning, 79–81
    packing materials, 15, 83–84, 197
    policies for, 77–79
Paints, 12
Pangea Organics, 10, 191

Paper
    for bags, 85
    recycled, 23, 70, 71
    waste prevention, 69–70, 158
Paperless meetings, 158
Paper-making process, 69, 71
Paper towels, 42
Parking lots, 191–192
Party waste, 108–109
Passive chilled beams, 49
Passive solar heating, 45–47
Patagonia, 166
Pax World Balanced Fund, 218
Pea straw, 84
Pepsi, 79
Peripherals, 91
Permeable paving, 191–192
Personal computers. *See* Computers
Personal information, 177
Pesticides, 167, 212
Petroleum. *See also* Vehicles
    all sources in carbon footprint, 10
    alternatives in printing inks, 72
    avoiding in cleaners, 115
    plastics made without, 134–135
    textiles made from, 167–168
    use in labels, 81
PHA packaging, 80
Philanthropy, encouraging, 200
Phillip Merrill Environmental Center, 183–184
Photocopies, 69, 70
Photoluminescent signs, 73
Pipes, insulating, 33, 34
Plants
    as indoor air filters, 65–66
    for rooftop gardens, 48
    using native, 60

Index

Plastics
    for bags, 85–87
    eco-friendly sources, 134–135
    recycling, 17–19
    reducing in packaging, 79, 83, 197
    vinyl signs, 73–74
Poland Spring, 79, 172
Policies
    packaging, 77–79
    purchasing, 23–24
    for setting thermostats, 31
Polluted sites, 188–190
Polyester, 167
Polyethylene terephthalate, 18
Polypropylene, 18
Polystyrene, 18
Polyvinyl chloride, 18
Popcorn, 84
Portfolio Manager, 9
Post-consumer recycled products, 14, 23
Poster boards, 73
Post-manufacturer recycled products, 14
Potted plants, 65–66
PowerFilm, 101
Power strips, 27
Prime Outlets mall, 192
Printer cartridges, 96
Printing, 69, 71–73
Procter & Gamble, 79
Products, greener, 131–133
Profits, sustainability and, 163, 233–234
Project Rejeaneration, 133
Promoting green practices, 171–174
Property owners, 189–190
Publications, 6
Public speaking, 173, 175, 227

Purchasing policies, 23–24
Pure fiber, 133

R

Racond, Annette, 210
Rainforest Alliance certification, 41
Rainwater, 63–65, 183–184
Ratings of window insulation, 35
Rayon, 168
Razor scooters, 175
Rechargeable batteries, 101–102
Reconstructed tires, 143
Recycled building materials, 183, 184, 185, 187–188
Recycling
    basic approaches, 14, 23
    carpet, 12
    computers, 96–97, 166
    consumer programs for, 165–167
    fabrics, 13, 166
    office programs, 16–17
    sorting plastics for, 17–19
    tires, 142–143
    waste sharing, 111–113
    wood products, 41
RecyclingCenters.org, 16
Redesigning packaging, 79–81
Regulations, lobbying for, 205–207
Renewable energy certificates, 152
Repositioning cruises, 125–126
Re-potting plants, 66
Restaurant noise pollution, 178–179
Retailer packaging policies, 78
Retirement funds, 217–219
Reuse
    bags, 85–87, 113
    beer bottle, 78
    in office remodeling, 12, 41
    shipping materials, 15, 25
    waste sharing, 111–113

Reverse osmosis filtering, 62
RideSpring, 146
River Rouge Plant, 48
Roadside assistance, 143–144
Rock wool insulations, 34
Role modeling, 201–202, 227–228
Roofs
    cooling, 47–48, 191
    saving rainwater from, 64
RPC Cresstale, 80

S

Safeco Insurance, 145
San Francisco Civic Tower, 184
Schools, speaking at, 227
Screen-printed labels, 82
Screensavers, 91
Seal-It, Inc., 82
Self-assessments, 225–226
Self-identifying information, 177
Seminars on sustainability, 173, 202
Sensors, light, 29
Shading devices, 45–46
Shared resources for offices, 37–38, 193
Shareholders, 219
Shipping materials, 15, 25, 124
Shipping practices, 128–129, 212
Shopping, 14–15
Shredding paper, 70
Shrink-film labels, 82
SIGG lifestyle bottles, 82
Signage, 73–74
Signatures, electronic, 98
Silicone caulk, 34
Silvercup Studios, 48
Sites.com, 209
Skylights, 46
Sleep mode, 91, 94
Soaps, 25

Social interactions, encouraging, 213–214
Socially responsible investing, 217–220
Social responsibility of suppliers, 124
Software
    computer energy use, 94
    eliminating packaging, 166
    Energy Star Portfolio Manager, 9
    enterprise asset management, 131
Solar energy
    active heating panels, 50–52
    battery chargers using, 101–102
    passive heating with, 45–47
Solar maps, 50
Solex, 112
Sonoco Sustainability Solutions, 107–108
Sorting plastics, 17–19
Soy-based inks, 72
Spam, 177
Speaking engagements, 173, 175, 227
Sponsorships, 198–201
Spray insulation, 33–34
Staff positions to oversee sustainability, 163–165, 228
Starbucks, 202
State incentives for telecommuters, 150
Stocks, 219
Stop the Junk Mail, 118
Stores
    downsizing, 193
    eco-friendly distribution, 126, 128–129
    noise pollution, 178–179

Index

Stores (*continued*)
  sustainable packaging in, 78,
    85–87
Strong, Roger, 50, 52–53
Styrofoam cups, 113
Styrofoam peanuts, 15, 83, 197
Subaru, 191
Suppliers
  environmentally sensitive,
    24–26, 123–125
  helping to become eco-friendly,
    202
  incentives for, 215
  seeking locally, 127–128
Supplies
  cooperative purchasing, 39
  purchasing policies for, 23–24
  selecting eco-friendly, 24–26
Surge protectors, 27
Surveys, 160, 176–178, 207–208
Sustainability officers, 163–165
Sustainability reports, 161–163
Sustainable brownfield regenera-
  tion, 189
Sustainable Forestry Initiative, 80
Sustainable packaging, 77–79. *See
  also* Packaging
Sustainable Packaging Coalition,
  78–79, 217
Synthetic textiles, 167–168
Szabo, Alex, 23

T
Taxes on plastic bags, 86
Teaching sustainability, 201–202,
  227–228
Teams
  building through community
    service, 198
  impact of sustainability on
    morale, 234

to promote eco-friendly prac-
  tices, 159–161
Teko Socks, 133
Telecommuting, 147–150
Teleconferencing, 150
Television, excessive, 178
Testimonials, 174
Textiles. *See* Clothing; Fabrics
Thegreenoffice.com, 23
Thermostats, 31, 32
Tierra Del Forte, 133
Timberland, 197–198
Time commitments, 5–7
Timing purchases, 24
Tires, 142–143
Title to properties, 189–190
Toshiba computers, 95
Tours, 227
Towels, 42
Toyota Prius hybrid, 141
Transparency, 215–217
Trash Talk shoes, 113
Travel, 144, 150–153
Treehugger, 151
Trees for the Future, 152
Trees For Travel, 152
Trial periods for telecommuters,
  149
2080 Program, 197
Two Mile Challenge, 199
Two-sided printing, 69

U
U-Factor, 35
ULPA filters, 116
Uniforms, 167
United States Climate Action Part-
  nership, 206
United States Green Building
  Council, 183, 188
UV air purifiers, 117

V

Vanpooling, 145

Vegetable-based inks, 72

Vehicles

    bio-plastics in, 134

    for business travelers, 151

    commuting alternatives, 145–147

    fuel efficient, 139–141

    greener tires for, 142–143

    roadside assistance, 143–144

Vendors

    environmentally sensitive, 123–125

    finding for recycling, 16

    seeking locally, 127–128

Ventilation

    in green buildings, 183–184

    promoting fresh air flow, 12–13

    skylights for, 46

    upgrading and maintaining, 30–32

Vents, 31, 37

Vermicomposting, 111

Videos, excessive, 178

Vinyl signs, 73–74

Viral marketing, 175

Voice mail, 102–103

Volatile organic compounds

    in building materials, 187

    in cleaners, 115

    in paints, 12

    in printing inks, 72

Volunteer hours for employees, 197–198

W

Wal-Mart, 78, 123

Waste audits, 107–108

Waste reduction, 16

Waste sharing, 111–113

Water conservation

    bathroom fixtures, 42

    practicing, 59–60

    by using rainwater, 63–65

Water coolers, 62

Water filtration, 61–63

Water heaters, 8, 34

Water pipes, 33, 34

Weatherizing covers, 36

Wellness, 209–210

The Wellness Track, 209–210

Whole building design, 187

Whole-house water filters, 62

Wilson, Sonsini, Goodrich & Rosati, 159, 160

Windows

    examining during energy audits, 8

    insulating and replacing, 34–36

    passive solar heating with, 46

Wind turbines, 52–54

WOMMA, 175–176

Wood products, certified eco-friendly, 13, 40–41

Wood shavings, 84

Wool, 167, 168

Word-of-mouth campaigns, 173, 174–176

WorldatWork, 147

Worm composting, 111

Woven bamboo, 54–55

Wrapping paper, 109

X

Xeriscaping, 191

Y

Yoga, 209

Z

Zipcar, 146

Zonbu computers, 95

Zoned systems, 30, 32

We See **Green**
In Your Future

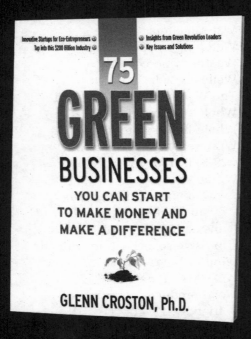

"*75 Green Businesses gets you quickly up to speed on the fast-paced trends propelling the green economy and shows you where to find the opportunities. If you're considering starting your own green business, Croston's book has practically written half your business plan for you. A terrific resource.*"

—Josh Dorfman, founder and CEO of Vivavi and author of *The Lazy Environmentalist*

"*Kermit is wrong! It's easy being green . . . Just read Croston's book. He provides a terrific guide to an amazing array of business eco-opportunities and tells you how to take advantage of them!*"

—Ray Smilor, executive director of the Beyster Institute of the Rady School of Management at University of California, San Diego, and author of *Daring Visionaries: How Entrepreneurs Build Companies, Inspire Allegiance and Create Wealth*

"*The biggest opportunities of the 21st century are green businesses. This wonderful book offers people who want to get involved a very comprehensive listing of those opportunities as well as numerous links to more information. Read it and get inspired.*"

—Greg Pahl, author of *The Citizen-Powered Energy Handbook: Community Solutions to a Global Crisis*

Discover **75 green** startup ideas in multiple industries, including ecotourism, small wind power, green schools, water conservation landscaping, green investment consulting and more!

Coming Soon!

Pick up your copy today!

AVAILABLE AT ALL FINE BOOKSTORES
AND ONLINE BOOKSELLERS
ENTREPRENEURPRESS.COM